Quarterly Essay

CONTENTS

Quarterly Essay is published four times a year by Black Inc., an imprint of Schwartz Publishing Pty Ltd. Publisher: Morry Schwartz.

ISBN 9781863951593 ISSN 1832-0953

Subscriptions – 1 year (4 issues): $49 within Australia incl. GST. Outside Australia $79.
2 years (8 issues): $95 within Australia incl. GST. Outside Australia $155.
Payment may be made by Mastercard, Visa or Bankcard, or by cheque made out to Schwartz Publishing. Payment includes postage and handling.

To subscribe, fill out and post the subscription card, or subscribe online at:

www.quarterlyessay.com

Correspondence and subscriptions should be addressed to the Editor at:

Black Inc. Level 5, 289 Flinders Lane
Melbourne VIC 3000 Australia
Phone: 61 3 9654 2000 / Fax: 61 3 9654 2290
Email:
quarterlyessay@blackincbooks.com (editorial)
subscribe@blackincbooks.com (subscriptions)

Editor: Chris Feik / Management: Sophy Williams
Publicity: Anna Lensky / Design: Guy Mirabella
Production Co-ordinator: Caitlin Yates

LOVE &
MONEY

The Family and
the Free Market

Anne Manne

"A princely marriage," observed the nineteenth-century essayist Walter Bagehot, "is a brilliant edition of a universal fact, and as such it rivets mankind." In the modern era, a political marriage is likely to interest us more than a princely one. While the royal family continues richly to reward us with the diverting antics of unemployed youths, retired grandmothers and wannabe princesses, it more resembles an exotic and morally chaotic soap opera – sex, infidelity and death – than offers a model for ordinary life. Unsurprisingly, then, we are more than ever likely to turn to our prominent political families as one guide – the "brilliant edition" – to contemporary relationships between men and women.

After Kevin Rudd won the leadership of the Australian Labor Party, it was not long before the nation's attention turned to his marriage with Therese Rein. As with John and Janette Howard, it was clear that this was a very strong partnership. However, if the Howards represented the old family model of breadwinner husband and homemaker wife, Kevin and Therese seemed to represent the new version: the dual-career power couple. Rein is an immensely successful businesswoman, whose enterprise, in helping the long-term unemployed, had developed from a two-person operation to a multi-million-dollar global business. The transition from the old to the new inhabitants of the Lodge quickly came to stand for more than a mere change of personnel. It was symbolic of the modernisation of the Australian family.

A politician must interest us to be successful. The mild-mannered, bespectacled man who self-deprecatingly called himself an unemployed diplomat held our attention. Kevin Rudd first interested me when I saw him tripping the light fantastic – doing the rumba – with Kerri-Anne Kennerley on her morning show. I immediately thought: he might win the next election. I was struck by his ease with women: he seemed to like women, and they liked him. If Rudd was good with women, it was because he gave the impression of being that most prized of creatures of female culture past and present: the good family man. From *Pride and Prejudice* to *Bridget Jones' Diary*, women who want children must sort the cads from the dads.

More is required of a good family man in the modern era than was required in John Howard's youth. Then it was enough that he be a good provider. Now our standards are higher: he must have a view of women capacious enough to include not only partnership in child-rearing as an involved and loving father, but respect for his spouse's independent endeavours in the public realm. He is part of a new social imagination about what love might mean between men and women.

Scarcely a week went by in the lead-up to the election without something turning up to interest us in the domestic life of the Rudds. In what was their political baptism of fire, a scandal erupted over the fact that Rein's company had inadvertently underpaid workers. They had been placed on precisely the kind of workplace contract that Rudd had been condemning. The scandal did not dent Rudd's popularity in the slightest. Deftly, he turned liability to advantage by speaking in the language of what family scholars call the new gender contract. He spoke with such respect for and pride in his wife's achievements that it solidified the impression of him as a loyal husband, and of the partnership as the updated version of companionate marriage. In the Rudd–Rein marriage, a space seemed to have been made for a woman to have her own career: "I've never asked Therese any time in the twenty-five years that I've been married to her that she should not be active in pursuing her dreams." They "had always supported each other." Rudd was "immensely proud of her achievements."

On closer inspection, however, the Therese and Kevin partnership tells us more about the contemporary patterns of Australian relationships than the commentariat, embracing them as the modern power couple, might have given us to understand. The complexity of their life history tells us why Rudd is able to dance so deftly, and simultaneously appeal as both an old- and new-fashioned family man.

This was made clear during the furore over his wife's business. Rudd made a bad gaffe. In defending Rein, he said that she was "an independent businesswoman rather than an appendage of middle-aged men." That instantly offended a great many Australians for a highly interesting reason. The old gender contract, of life-long separate spheres for male breadwinner and homemaker wife, is no longer universal. Yet if motherhood as a monolith, a hegemonic idea, as one life path, is breaking up, in the new scenario women are replacing the old patterns of the past with not just one, but several patterns. (This helps to explain the continual outbreaks of the "mother wars" over which pattern of child-rearing is right.) A minority of families have two full-time workers along the dual-career model. Another minority have a breadwinner husband and homemaker wife. Far more families have a primary and secondary earner. In what the British sociologist of women's work, Catherine Hakim, has called the "adaptive pattern," one parent, usually but not always the mother, shapes their working life around the needs of children. In this pattern, women overwhelmingly work part time in preference to full time. Many spend at least some time as a stay-at-home mum while their children are small.

Any politician straddles not only the old world and the new, but also this fraught, complex and conflict-ridden world of choice. It is easy to make a mis-step and offend someone, because we are all doing it differently. Rudd and Rein are not, in fact, the pure embodiment of work-centred careerists whose dilemmas of baby versus briefcase so preoccupy our commentariat, most of whom are themselves leading that life. The occasional columnist for the *Age*, Natasha Cica, for example, claimed that as a millionaire businesswoman,

> Rein is pretty stock standard – most able-bodied Australian mothers work, or they want to. As is her husband – most able-minded Australian men don't want a dependent appendage and are prepared to stand up and say so. So why the fevered commentary pitch?

In fact, Therese stayed home when her first two children were small, supporting Kevin in his diplomatic career, following him to Sweden and then China. That makes her a member of Hakim's "adaptive" group, rather than straightforwardly work-centred. Nor did the Rudds share Cica's contempt for stay-at-home mothers. Defending Rudd against accusations that he had insulted such women, Rein said:

> There was a period of time where I was a stay-at-home mum and he fully supported me. There are a whole range of choices that people make in life and a whole range of things that people have to juggle. I have been a mum with two young kids and juggling all of that, I have enormous respect for the people in that position.

Rudd, the Labor populist who had spent a lot of time in the shopping centres of his Queensland electorate getting in touch with ordinary voters, quickly corrected himself. This time he spoke in the "chart your own course" language of postmodern individualism and choice, where, as Anthony Giddens has observed, there is no fixed model for the good life.

> What I was saying yesterday was that women must have the right to choose, the right to choose to be a stay-at-home mum, the right to

choose to nurture a home, or the right to choose to go to work or to build their own professional career ... We have been through that entire spectrum of life experiences ourselves, where with little kids Therese has been at home, building up a home. Then starting off on her own career some time after that.

Yet, further confounding the stereotypes, before a conservative might sigh with relief and define Rein as "serious" about her family but blessedly "unserious" about a little job on the side, it quickly became clear that for her, work is a deeply felt vocation.

What I do at work is my life support ... It's a mission for me to help people who are highly disadvantaged back into jobs that are lasting and decent. It's a lifeline for me [just as] for Kevin politics is not a career, but this is not a battle for dominance, or power or money, it's about purpose.

The key to the passion she felt about such work lay in the past. Her father, to whom she was very close, was an aeronautical engineer. He had been crippled when a plane he was testing during the Second World War crashed. Wheelchair-bound, he was nonetheless determined to work and succeeded in doing so, except for brief periods when he took the disability pension. Crucial to the story was the role taken by Therese Rein's mother, supporting and encouraging:

I know that when you have someone alongside you saying, "I think you can" – which is what my mum did for my dad, she was the urger, she was the encourager – when that's happening, people can do the extra-ordinary ... He wanted to work. I suppose that's where I learnt about the importance of work in people's lives.

By the affair's end, the potential First Couple had done something quite unusual in Australian politics. They had spoken about family and working life in a way that seemed to pay tribute to both, and not diminish either.

The rigid divisions of the work and family debate, the cruel "either you are for me or against me" gusto with which one was flung into one or other camp, were overturned. It seemed suddenly possible that the work/life collision might give way to a welcome reconciliation of family and working life. Just for a moment, the intolerant atmosphere of the interminable mother wars seemed laid to rest, and a vision put forward which was generous enough to include everyone.

Unhappily, however, it was a rare moment.

In the United States in late 2005, the retired trial lawyer, legal academic and feminist Linda Hirshman made a striking intervention in the mother wars. Writing in the magazine *The American Prospect*, Hirshman attacked educated women for their part in the so-called "opt-out revolution." This term referred to a 13 per cent rise in the number of new mothers staying home with babies. The controversy was over the question of choice. Did such women freely choose home and children? Or was workplace inflexibility and the absence of affordable child-care creating a situation more "lock-out" than "opt-out"?

Hirshman decided to investigate. She interviewed thirty women who had announced their engagements in the up-market magazine *New York Times Style*. While her sample was not, admittedly, the most exhaustive survey of American womanhood, Hirshman announced that the trend was indeed true. One interviewee would not come to the phone to answer questions because she was baking apple pie. Another "had a wedding to plan." It was time to intervene.

In the no-nonsense tone of my old hockey mistress, who clapped her hands on a freezing morning and shouted at the panting team, "Girls, girls, pull your socks up and run another lap!", Hirshman outlined "The Rules." A bemused *Guardian* reporter summed them up like this: "put work first, marry beneath you, and never have more than one child." Women must not marry for love. They must drive a hard bargain on housework, getting the upper hand by training up and marrying down (to lower-status men who have flexible work lives and can therefore take the mummy track themselves). Women must pursue self-interest at every point:

> The best way to treat work seriously is to find the money. Money is the marker of success in a market economy; it usually accompanies power, and it enables the bearer to wield power, including within the family.

Hirshman questioned the sacrosanct notion of the age: the individual's freedom to choose. The sad legacy of liberal feminism, she argued, had been to bequeath to us this destructive ideal:

> Here's the feminist moral analysis that [the] choice [to stay at home] avoided: The family – with its repetitious, socially invisible, physical tasks – is a necessary part of life, but it allows fewer opportunities for full human flourishing than public spheres like the market or the government ... To paraphrase, as Mark Twain said, "A man who chooses not to read is just as ignorant as a man who cannot read."

Such choices, she went on,

> are bad for women individually. A good life for humans includes the classical standard of using one's capacities for speech and reason in a prudent way, the liberal requirement of having enough autonomy to direct one's own life, and the utilitarian test of doing more good than harm in the world. Measured against these time-tested standards, the expensively educated upper-class moms will be leading lesser lives ... these daughters of the upper classes will be bearing most of the burden of the work always associated with the lowest caste: sweeping and cleaning bodily waste ... They have voluntarily become untouchables.

Whether Hirshman was quite measuring up to her "classical standard of using one's capacities for speech and reason in a prudent way" or the "utilitarian test of doing more good than harm in the world," one thing at least was certain. She gave a whole new meaning to the old joke: "Before the feminist revolution, housewives were second-class citizens. Afterwards, they were subhuman!"

As the controversy over her views gathered strength, Hirshman threw a wider net. If fury from humiliated at-home mommy bloggers and conservative opinion columnists was not surprising, she soon clashed with those with progressive politics who worked from home or had taken a temporary break to care for children. They, too, by not fulfilling ideal worker norms, experienced the lash of her tongue. She read their blogs about their lives and pronounced them uninteresting. Taken together, the women she attacked constituted most American mothers.

Soon she had a blog, a book contract and the kind of notoriety that brings with it appearances on *Sixty Minutes* and *Good Morning America*. The reporter from the *Guardian* discovered:

> She loves work. She believes in work. "To build a life out of the things that aren't work is like eating cream puffs for every meal," she proclaims. She is convinced that a truly flourishing life is impossible without paid employment. Her moments of fulfilment came in 1978, when she racked up 2,700 billable hours as a labour lawyer, and in 1984, when she was part of a team of lawyers arguing a case before the supreme court.

If Hirshman's valuation of work reflected her own life practice, so too did her feelings about caring for babies. Getting her metaphors a little muddled, after likening child-rearing to a diet of cream puffs, she then likened it to being a Nazi torture victim:

> [Hirshman] is sceptical about the premise of maternity leave – never having really seen the need for it personally – and worries that women who take a career pause immediately after giving birth expose all women to charges of unreliability. The notion of maternal baby bonding does not appear to enter into her thinking. "You know what maternity leave is really good for?" she asks. "You are constantly getting awakened in the night and so you feel like the victim of a Nazi experiment – how long can this woman go without sleep and still function. That's a physical thing."

In the unruly but nonetheless democratic space of the blogosphere, humiliated mothers of all stripes got their own back. It was a different story at the New York Times, Boston Globe, Washington Post, Salon.com and Slate. While Hirshman complained in an injured tone in the New York Times, "Everyone Hates Linda!" what struck me when viewing the firestorm of comment was how favourably the commentariat responded. Sure, she was a little extreme, seemed to be the general view, but didn't she have a point?

Farewell to Maternalism

What did it mean, the Hirshman kerfuffle? One way of seeing it – as yet another salvo in the mother wars – is not very illuminating. What is illuminating is the title of the short book Hirshman published in 2006, developing her ideas: Get to Work: a Manifesto for Women of the World. Hirshman may put her points with a distinctively gleeful, insulting cruelty, but her position is not far distant from the covert ideology of not only the US government but also bodies like the OECD, the European Union, the World Bank and the International Monetary Fund. All see economic advantages to increasing women's participation in the workforce, all advocate "post-maternalist" policies that involve cutting financial assistance for maternal care of children and redirecting it to day-care. The title of one OECD report captures the mood: Putting More Women to Work.

That message, it will be argued here, is the core element of a shift affecting all Western societies. It is a new paradigm.

"Across the rich, developed democracies of Western Europe, North America and the Antipodes, we are in the midst of a series of what might be called 'farewells to maternalism,'" writes Ann Orloff. Countries are moving from a "maternalist" policy model, under which mothers were expected to stay home full time with their children and eschew employment, to a model of "employment for all," in which women are expected to enter the labour force, but with the assumption that they will continue to provide or organise household care.

In most countries, Orloff goes on to observe, "housewifery is in serious, possibly terminal decline." The majority of women, including mothers of young children, are in the workforce. Claims to state support for mothering and other forms of caregiving are under challenge. Poor mothers in the US, for example, can no longer count on government aid. Rather they are expected to be self-supporting – in some states as early as three months after childbirth. It is not only women's own changed expectations that are driving the shift:

> The farewell to maternalism has been very much encouraged by ... state authorities [who] are ... motivated by more mundane considerations. With birth-rates well below replacement level, and the baby-boom generation approaching retirement age, labor is slated to turn into a shortage ... [more workers are needed] to cover the pension entitlements owed to the swelling cohort of retirees.

In Australia, too, such considerations dominate. The Treasury's *Intergenerational Report* centred on the issue of falling fertility. As fewer children are born, the working-age population shrinks while the number of those its taxes supports – children, young mothers caring for children, the sick, disabled and, in particular, older people – swells. Even under the socially conservative Howard government, Peter Costello's budgets centred on boosting workforce participation by making "active" those previously inactive. There is no reason to think Wayne Swan's priorities will be any different.

Mobilising labour to balance the national accounts is labelled "social inclusion." For example, on the eve of the 2007 election Costello extolled the virtues of "using the tools of economic strength" to help those previously "excluded from work's bounty." He identified diabetics and manic-depressives, who, Costello maintained, had recently been beneficiaries of (unspecified) breakthroughs in treatment. Putting sick people to work was an instance of "social inclusion." On another occasion, Costello claimed he wanted to make Australia the most "woman-friendly" nation in the world. This turned out to mean providing more work and more child-care.

Few in the commentariat doubt that this indeed represents women's universal interest. Ken Davidson, for example, writing election commentary, said:

> Both the Government and the Opposition want to get women back into the workforce as quickly as possible after giving birth. I suspect that most mothers are also keen on getting back into paid employment as soon as possible.

The new model is that women must undertake paid work ("employment for all") *as well as* caregiving. Only economically "active" adults will be supported. To varying degrees, the expectation is that women will be granted brief leaves of absence – around childbirth, for example. But they will be expected to engage in life-long, as close as possible to full-time, work. As Catherine Hakim points out:

> [The] research reports and policy papers of international bodies such as the European Commission (EC) and the International Labour Office (ILO) repeatedly endorse the proposition that all women want to work continuously throughout life.

In Australia, the quality press regularly expresses views similar in content if not in tone to Hirshman's. One headline in 2005 screamed "Costello: Get Mums Working," conveying the Treasurer's blunt instruction to single mothers to return to work. One newspaper editorial said point-blank that mothers are more valuable to society as workers than as stay-at-home mums. If Hirshman has decided on behalf of women that their best interests lie in the workplace, and in compelling women to work, she is not alone. The *Australian*'s George Megalogenis, writing of measures to reduce support for single mothers, said, "welfare-to-work reform has the *noble* goal of *pushing* single mums back into the labour force" (my italics). A local Hirshmanite, Leslie Cannold, sternly told *Age* readers that women "ought not have a choice," and should be forced to return to work as soon as their babies were "out of nappies."

Those shaping the elite cultural script – such as the Australian Institute of Family Studies, the Human Rights and Equal Opportunities Commission, the 2006 Senate Inquiry into balancing work and family, the *Intergenerational Report*, the Treasury, university staff, economists, government departments and research units, and, in particular, early-childhood faculties, all accept Hirshman's basic premise: women should Get to Work! They just put the case more politely.

Why does it matter? What is wrong with the Get to Work program? Surely, it is what all women now want? Isn't that what "equality" is all about?

Not so fast.

The women's movement was one of several transcendent movements for justice which emerged in the '60s. Together these movements overturned our longstanding assumptions about human hierarchy: white over black, men over women.

In pursuing equality and justice, the women's movement sought equal opportunities in education, public and economic life. Business and the professions were entirely dominated by men; there were no female newsreaders, few female politicians. The ideology of separate spheres – public life for men and private life for women – had installed the norm of the ideal worker. All work was shaped by the assumption of a wife off-field to take care of dependents and the household. A "good worker" was someone who could work long hours, unencumbered by family responsibilities. This last aspect of the old gender contract is at the very heart of why family and work conflict.

The achievements of liberal feminism, in a few short decades, have been nothing short of remarkable. Its proponents overturned an all-but-compulsory homemaker and motherhood role; the longstanding rule that married women resign on marriage from the public service was done away with. Liberal feminism has resulted in a version of emancipation that can be roughly translated as equal rights for women in the workplace.

"Equality" is interpreted as meaning sameness with men – hence all the anxious assessments on International Women's Day comparing pay-rates, number of female parliamentarians and female board members, and so on. Yet making the workplace the arena of women's liberation, important as that is, does not in any way challenge the ideal worker norms that make it so difficult for women to combine motherhood and work. Indeed, the Linda Hirshmans of this world strengthen such norms even further by asserting them as ideals for women as well as men.

Feminism is divided on motherhood and women's unpaid labour. Some feminists – "care" feminists – share the liberal goal of opening up work opportunities for women, but feel, as Jane Waldfogel put it, that "equality as sameness has got us so far but not far enough." As things stand, it will never deliver equality for more than an elite few.

In fact, their concerns go deeper than this. As Raimond Gaita has observed, the '60s liberation movements expressed a desire for justice that went beyond equality of opportunity: "Treat me as a person; see me fully as a human being, as fully your equal, without condescension ... These are calls to justice conceived as an equality of respect." Hirshman's harsh denigration of women who centre their lives on caregiving shows that a narrow, reductive interpretation of equal opportunity does nothing to answer that deeper call for justice.

By contrast, care feminists see the devaluation and economic marginalisation of caregiving work as an essential aspect of women's oppression. Revaluing such care in symbolic and practical ways is central to the liberation project. After all, denigrating caregivers as a "caste of untouchables" does not enhance our respect for the women who still do most of this labour – whether they work for pay or not. Nor does it tempt men to do more of it.

With respect to motherhood, care feminists feel Hirshman and co. are guilty of throwing the baby out with the bathwater. As Ann Crittenden says, one cannot lump "the care of the children with all the other menial labour women were assigned, as if child-care were equivalent to dishwashing, and as if women could flee their children as easily as they could run away from dirty laundry." Devaluing motherhood – still central in so many women's lives – does feminism no favours. The victory of one path (sameness feminism) offers only partial solutions and is, in the end, fatally flawed.

Of the two paths, however, thus far it has been the Get to Work route to women's equality that has been hailed as the true representative of women's emancipation. The reason for this, however, has less to do with it being the only worthwhile version of feminism and more to do with its compatibility with the new economy.

THE FEMINIST ETHIC AND THE SPIRIT OF THE NEW CAPITALISM

In his classic essay "The Protestant Ethic and the Spirit of Capitalism," Max Weber showed how one variant of Christianity, Protestantism, emerged as the key legitimating idea of early capitalism. With Catholicism, salvation was assured by submission to the Church's authority. With Calvinist Protestantism, God's grace was less certain. Protestants could only fathom whether they were fulfilling God's will, and would become one of the Elect, by measuring their progress in material terms. In this way, pious churchmen felt vindicated and assured of heavenly reward when they achieved worldly success.

Central to the Protestant ethic was the notion of work as a vocation. If work was part of God's great design, it was more than just a job – it was a calling. Work was thus imbued with a heavenly glow. It had a profound *moral* significance. In attaching a sacramental quality to the humblest occupations in the secular world, and to the most profane of tasks – making money – an extraordinary productivity was unleashed. Since Puritanism also forbade conspicuous consumption, the ethos of delayed gratification gave a potent rationale for saving rather than spending. It encouraged the rational pursuit of economic gain.

Weber's thesis has a strongly paradoxical aspect: one system of ideas ends up fuelling the success of another, despite being foreign to it. While the development of capitalism was never the aim of Protestantism, as a belief system it fostered a unique constellation of human values and qualities which helped create the conditions for a capitalist economy to flourish.

Weber has been interpreted as drawing attention to the significance of ideas in the making of history, against Marx who emphasised the underlying economic interests of the ruling class. Yet Weber's analysis is more subtle than that. He points to the intertwining of the two things:

> Not ideas, but material and ideal interests, directly govern men's conduct. Yet very frequently the "world images" that have been

> created by "ideas" have, like switchmen, determined the tracks
> along which action has been pushed by the dynamic of interest.

Ideas can act like "switchmen," determining the tracks along which history runs. But ideas are also pushed forward and transformed by the "dynamic of interest." And certain ideas, or strands, may be left behind. This applies to social movements as well as religious ones.

Upon what tracks have feminist ideas run? The answer is: market tracks. In the 1970s, stagflation – a combination of unemployment and inflation – saw capitalism hover on the brink of crisis. This was the death knell of Keynesian economics and of the welfare state, which had supported capitalism's golden age. But then two new prophets emerged – neo-liberalism and feminism.

It is vital to see that two revolutions – the transformation of women's roles and great resurgence of free-market ideals – occurred at the very same moment in history. As Barbara Pocock notes, the women's movement's long-overdue struggle to open up equal opportunities in the workplace "found its happy co-conspirator in a market greedy for women's labour, its 'flexibility,' and enthusiastic for the spending power of women's earnings. Of all of feminism's goals, entry to paid work has been the most compatible with the globalising market."

Here, then, lies the answer as to why it was the Get to Work version of feminism which was hailed as the legitimate voice of women's emancipation. It is easy to see why it is so compatible with neo-liberal economics. Both liberal feminism and the new capitalism shared an insistence on employment as having a *moral* significance, and placed it at the very centre of their grand narrative of progress. There is no intrinsic contradiction between the needs of corporate capitalism and the upper-middle-class professional couple. As Jean Bethke Elshtain puts it, Betty Friedan's famous *The Feminine Mystique* "was a paean in praise of the rat race – she just wanted women to join it."

Yet here we strike a similar paradox to that noted by Weber in relation to Protestantism and capitalism. In entering into a "dangerous liaison" with the new capitalism, feminism has been distorted – put to work to lend legitimacy to very different interests. As Arlie Hochschild puts it, feminism has been abducted:

> Just as Protestantism, according to Max Weber, "escaped from the cage" of the Church to be transposed into an inspirational "spirit of capitalism" that drove men to make money and build capitalism, so feminism may be "escaping the cage" of a social movement to buttress a commercial spirit of intimate life that was originally separate from and indeed alien to it.

*

The "new capitalism" is a term coined by Richard Sennett to refer to the great leap forward into the globalised, hyper-competitive, free-market economy. It has delivered remarkable economic growth and prosperity. Anglo-American societies have transformed themselves from economies based on industrial-age manufacturing to service-based, high-consumption ones. The old Australian settlement has been swept aside. Protectionism is a thing of the past, as is centralised wage-fixing. There is a sharpened imperative to compete under globalisation, creating a new "risk society." Labour shedding and efforts to raise productivity have led to an intensification of work, and pressure to hold down labour costs. If the recognisable human face of the old regime was a male factory worker, for the new capitalism it is a female service employee, such as a child-care or aged-care worker.

There is a shift not just of economic activity but of sensibility, away from the ethic of delayed gratification and towards the hedonism of a service-oriented consumer society. "Affluenza," the luxury fever of conspicuous consumption, means that our homes are overflowing with new gadgets, and that there are now more than 1000 self-storage sites around Australia where we can stash our excess stuff. Average income is now three times what it was in the 1950s. Houses in the US are now twice as big as in the 1950s and have twice as many bathrooms as in the 1970s. In Australia, as average house size swelled to 250 square metres, the average number of people within them shrank to 2.6.

Family life is being reshaped in the new economy. Although it is rarely made explicit, the new capitalism is contingent on a trade-off: higher productivity is translated not into more time at home but more hours worked per family per year to service our consumption habit. Unprecedented levels of indebtedness lead to a work-and-spend cycle, with more family hours going into paid work. The two-income family is also a "hedge fund" against the risk society. One OECD publication explains:

> Social policies based on the male-breadwinner model of the family have become outmoded … female labour-market participation provides a form of self-insurance to households, with the income risks attached to involuntary non-employment reduced … [The dual-income family] serves as a risk hedge against periods of un-employment.

In the new capitalism, work has become sacred. The title of a recent book summed it up: *Better Than Sex: How a Whole Generation Got Hooked on Work*. Work has taken on an enchanted quality, and the emotional poles of home and workplace "are in the process of being reversed." Both left and right have got religion on this matter. The economics columnist Ross Gittins noted bemusedly of Peter Costello's 2007 budget that it was all about the "sanctification of work."

> It was written all over last month's federal budget, but nobody could see it. I missed it myself. And it wouldn't surprise me if the very authors of the budget missed its significance. Why did every-one miss it? Because it's become so commonplace. It's just what you'd expect economists and politicians to be on about. What was

it? Work. Work and more work. The budget was obsessed by work. Those who aren't working, should be. Those who are working, aren't working hard enough. And those considering retirement should resist the temptation.

Don Edgar, the former head of the Australian Institute of Family Studies, might be counted on to put an alternative view. But no. "We have to work," explained Edgar, "to make us fully human." The left-leaning elite are singing the same tune as the right.

What our enchantment with material progress, affluence and the ideal of work obscures, however, is the paradox of progress. Weber remarked how capitalism could become "an iron cage." We have created a new version of that cage. In their 2003 book *The Two-Income Trap*, Elizabeth Warren and Amelia Warren Tyagi described how a greater proportion of the American middle class was going bankrupt than ever before. The crucial variable was children.

In the United States, tax cuts to the wealthy are financed by running down state services, such as education, while the cost of private health insurance has escalated. Under a user-pays system, Warren and Tyagi found, parents spent far more on basics, including housing in a good school district, education, college fees and health-care. They earned more, but they also had to pay more for everything. Hence more and more middle-class families sent Mum into the workforce, just to keep pace and try to maintain a foothold in the middle class. Yet this simply created a bidding war for the core items, such as housing and education, of a middle-class life. The two-income family "ratcheted up the price of a middle-class life for everyone, including families that wanted to keep Mom at home."

In Australia, while we still have important elements of an older social-democratic model (such as Medicare), similar problems are emerging. As government funding of state institutions is run down, many middle-class families feel that the best health and education are obtained by purchasing private health cover and private schooling. In recent years we have seen a housing affordability crisis, as investors have responded to negative-gearing incentives by entering into a bidding war. By 2006 the average Australian mortgage was around $1300 a month. Many families paid more, with just under 10 per cent paying $3000 a month or more. And, as with America, the purchasing power of the two-income family drove up prices for everyone.

It is this paradox of progress that explains John Howard's defeat at a time of economic boom. The Howard government attempted to broker an implausible marriage between the animal spirits of an unfettered capitalism and social conservatism. What Howard did not see was the essential tension between the two. As Anthony Giddens has remarked, "individualism and choice are supposed to stop abruptly at the boundaries of the family and national identity. But nothing is more dissolving of tradition than the permanent revolution of market forces." Hence, despite Howard's personal sympathy for single-income families and stay-at-home mothers, high levels of indebtedness and dramatically spiralling house prices propelled mothers into the workforce.

The Howard era saw the work/life collision move to centre-stage. In bookshops, shelves creaked under the weight of a new genre: *The Second Shift*; *The Time Bind*; *When Work Doesn't Work Anymore*; *Crowded Lives*; *I Don't Know How She Does It*. All deal with the new scarcity of time in working families. Howard famously declared this issue the "great barbecue stopper," but then did little about it.

Incredibly, instead of responding to the family needs of the new workforce, he introduced the harsh WorkChoices legislation, pushing the neo-liberal revolution even further. It proved his undoing. Australians delivered a decisive repudiation of Howard's belief in the perfect match between the neo-liberal workplace and a flourishing family life. The reasons why are easily demonstrated.

In their report *An Unexpected Tragedy*, Relationships Australia found substantial evidence linking the new working patterns of families with relationship breakdown and poor outcomes for children. At a time when 60 per cent of couples with children under fifteen had both parents employed, Australians also began working longer hours. The land of the long weekend was rapidly transformed. Alongside the US, New Zealand and Japan, Australia now puts in the longest hours among OECD nations. More than 20 per cent of workers work fifty hours per week or more. In social-democratic Sweden and Finland, the figure is less than 5 per cent. The percentage of the Australian workforce working between forty-five and sixty hours per week has increased by almost 100 per cent since 1978.

Unsociable and atypical hours (night time, early mornings and week-ends) increased too. By 1997, 75 per cent of men and 47 per cent of women did some work during atypical hours. During the 1990s, the pro-portion of people working on Sundays increased from less than 14 per cent of the workforce in 1974 to more than 23 per cent in 1997, while 35 per cent worked on Saturdays. Regular overtime increased, with more than half of fathers with children under twelve working overtime. Women workers doing manual or unskilled labour were more likely to be working early mornings, the key time to get children off to child-care or school.

The evidence is clear that the weekends are when families spend most time together. When mothers as well as fathers work during the week, carving out some unhurried family time on weekends is important. Yet parents who worked on Sundays lost six hours of interaction time with children. The other partner did not make up that time. It was, quite sim-ply, time lost.

Insecure employment also increased. So did part-time work. Casual employment rose to 24 per cent of the workforce. Australia has the second highest growth-rate of temporary employees in the OECD. It is the only nation with the dubious distinction of combining long hours – over one-fifth of all employees work more than fifty hours per week – with very high levels of casualisation. *An Unexpected Tragedy* presents evidence to show that the more insecure the employment, the worse the mental health of the employee.

The strain on working mothers has been especially intense. Working mothers responded by devoting great energy to spending time with children on top of their multiple responsibilities. They sacrificed leisure time and personal care in the process. Nonetheless, despite such efforts, a mother's time with her children was reduced by about twenty-five minutes for every hour worked. Just under half of the working mothers surveyed reported that they did not have enough time.

The effect on children of parents working longer and atypical hours is troubling. Research is very clear on the detrimental effects of a mother's depression on long-term outcomes for children, and these new working patterns make depression more likely. Overworked parents are more likely to be angry, inconsistent or ineffective. Children whose parents worked atypical hours were more likely to suffer increased separation anxiety, to become more physically aggressive and to have problems of hyperactivity and inattention. Younger children and those from lower socio-economic backgrounds suffer the most.

What all this research shows is that the resounding rejection of Work-Choices was no accident. More than two-thirds of Australians think our working hours are too long. Almost two-thirds of those working long hours believe it interferes with their family life. More than half of those working forty-five hours or more want to reduce hours. Between 1992 and 2002, just under a fifth of Australians downshifted, trading less work for more time.

When both sides of politics continually refer to "working families," it clearly speaks to a sense of grievance. The pressure, however, is often as much from the "time bind" and being locked into the work-and-spend cycle as from economic hardship. John Howard's pre-election boast that "working families have never had it so good" went down like the proverbial lead balloon. The rhetoric of "working families doing it tough," even when some in reality have high incomes, evokes a psychological aspect of the new family life. It speaks to those who are income-rich but mortgaged up to the eyeballs, and who instead suffer "time poverty" as a result of both parents working longer hours.

We are at an historic turning point in the relationship between family and work. We need a new Australian settlement, a societal deal brokered between government, business, unions and Australian families. With the defeat of the Howard government and the election of a Rudd Labor government, that new deal is possible. Yet we remain finely poised, between an intolerant Get to Work program and a more inclusive pathway, which recognises and supports the important work of caregiving as well as paid work.

Thus far in Australia, huge emphasis has been placed on the Human Rights and Equal Opportunity Commission's campaign for paid maternity leave and the Howard government's refusal to provide it. Fourteen weeks of paid maternity leave became a symbol of Howard's innate conservatism and his refusal to face the alleged realities of modern families. The commentariat was in permanent uproar.

Paid maternity leave around childbirth is surely an essential human need. Yet, in the light of the much more generous policies elsewhere, the Australian proposal looks spectacularly limited. Other societies, such as Britain and Canada, are following Scandinavia's example in providing longer paid leaves. Most of Europe does likewise, granting more generous paid-leave entitlements than a mere fourteen weeks. Moreover, most nations, to help boost fertility, include at-home mothers in family-support schemes. The Human Rights and Equal Opportunity Commission's proposal, by contrast, left out those mothers who were not in the labour force at the time of giving birth. And then there is the larger problem. After the first fourteen weeks of a baby's life, parents need to balance family and work for another eighteen years or more!

Betty Friedan once told Simone de Beauvoir that she believed women should have the choice to stay home to raise their children if that is what they wished to do. De Beauvoir answered, "No, we don't believe that any woman should have this choice. No woman should be authorised to stay home to raise her children. Society should be totally different. Women should not have that choice, precisely because if there is such a choice, too many women will make that one."

The old breadwinner/homemaker family was enforced by legislation, discrimination and everyday norms. Our historical closeness to that regime, however, makes us slow to recognise that we can install the new gender contract – the "farewell to maternalism" – with a bloody-minded coerciveness. What is so striking among the partisans for the Get to Work program is the breathtaking complacency with which they regard state coercion.

Women's autonomy over balancing work and family – such intimate matters as birthing, breastfeeding, the speed of physical and psychological separation of mother and child and the timing of the return to work – is treated with blithe disregard. Where once the feminist movement rose up in unison to oppose state coercion, it is now not uncommon for the work-centred commentariat to view such coercion with placid equanimity, as being for "her own good." Usually the coerciveness is subtle: a vanguard of well-intentioned new gender wardens insist where women's "true" interests lie, invariably in living lives like their own! The entirely legiti-mate needs of the career-focused mother are assumed to be universal. Then claims can be made for exclusive government funding for the favoured group.

David McKnight, who spent time as a stay-at-home dad, saw this as a flaw in Anne Summers' book *The End of Equality*:

> the core of Summers' vision is that equality for women means identical participation in paid work for women and men. It is a career-focused feminism. Equality means sameness and any varia-tion from this road must be avoided. She therefore assumes that any break from paid work should be as brief as possible. Government

support for child-care to allow women to remain in paid work must on principle take priority over government support for full-time mothers to care for their children.

McKnight also notes that the high-profile demographer Peter McDonald, who frequently advises government committees, after a cursory survey of opinion polls, including one showing about a third of respondents preferred traditional family arrangements, said "social institutions have been subjected to the goals of feminism but the family is lagging behind."

But if the people are lagging behind, behind whom, precisely? When De Beauvoir says, "we don't believe that any woman should have this choice," just who is the "we" here? And what do women want?

THERE'S NO PLACE LIKE WORK?

At one time in my life I had permanently singed fingertips. Between my final year at school and university, I had my first job. It was in outback New South Wales. I was, as it was quaintly called, a jillaroo, a general stationhand who rounded up cattle and worked on the farm. To this the prim advertisement in the country paper the *Weekly Times* had added: "some domestic duties." After a long, hot trip on a train, I arrived on a deserted platform surrounded by flat, red and dusty terrain stretching out for miles in every direction. The station owner met me, and looked me up and down doubtfully through narrowed eyes.

As matters turned out, I was less jillaroo than live-in domestic slave. Working the cattle under Mr Slavedriver (as I soon christened my boss) was by far the best, but unhappily by far the least, of my job. Usually, to beat the pulsing summer heat, the stockmen and I would go out in the dark before dawn to round up the stock for market. We rode rough but nimble stockhorses, cutting out cattle and herding the reluctant beasts into yards. Then our job was to climb into the yards, and on foot persuade unruly cows that their best hope was to go to market. Few of them agreed. We finished each morning's work with red dust clogging our boots and coating our skins. It was tough and dirty work, leavened by exhilarating gallops cracking a stockwhip overhead to round up breakaways from the mob.

Stock work was finished at around 8 a.m. Then it was time to begin work for Mrs Slavedriver. That part of the job went on until about 9 p.m. I cooked every meal for the family, did all the housework to exacting standards, washed all the clothes, including the baby's nappies, did the ironing and fed all the domestic animals. My last task was dragging heavy kerosene tins full of bread and wet slops 100 metres up a steep hill to the cattle dogs tied up on a bleak ridge.

Some days, at the end of a sixteen-hour shift, I thought I would never get to the top. I would stand, swaying, at the bottom of the hill, looking at the sharp incline ahead, feeling the tug of the tin cans weighing down on my shoulders. Since then I have only rarely felt the depth of exhaustion that I felt every day.

But why the burnt fingertips? Mrs Slavedriver had an odd quirk. Although this was a large and prosperous station, she could not bear to waste matches. "Outrageous extravagance!" she called it. She would fly into a rage over the thought of a matchstick used only once. So I would re-use matches, over and over, until they burnt right to the stump, burning my fingertips on the way.

Each summer I had similarly dismal jobs. The next was at a racehorse stable riding trackwork and mucking out boxes, before I moved up in the world to selling encyclopaedias door to door, followed by many stints of waitressing in downmarket hamburger joints and upmarket cafes. In a grim kind of way, I quite enjoyed parts of these jobs. I can still instantly conjure a memory of charging down hill wielding a stockwhip, or galloping a thoroughbred on the track. Physical labour has its own kind of pride – in the sheer act of endurance. I harbour no nostalgia, however, for any of the indoor jobs. Those jobs gave me some money of my own, a supplement to scholarship funds. But all of them were made bearable only by one simple fact. They came to an end. I was there for the summer, and then I was out of there.

The kinds of jobs I did convinced me not of Linda Hirshman's maxim, that the key to the meaning of life is work, but of Winston Churchill's. He thought the world was divided into two classes of people: a minority of people who work at jobs they like – and the rest. There are people who live to work, and there are people who work in order to live.

After child-rearing I started to write. Meeting deadlines can be arduous, but I can now earn a living doing something I love. I often have a sneaking, guilty thought, *and one is paid to do this!* One day I walked out into the sunshine with my publisher, after a sparkling lunch at an excellent restaurant. She said, "And we call this work!"

Quite.

When, fresh from my life as a stationhand and domestic worker, I encountered from my university teachers the standard belief that paid work was the key to the meaning of life, I was politely incredulous. When they spoke about work, the word had a resonance, even an Eros to it. It sounded powerful, glamorous and full of purpose, bestowing the good life. They meant prestige jobs, the kind Betty Friedan advocated in *The Feminine Mystique*:

> the only kind of work which permits an able woman to realise her abilities ... [is] the lifelong commitment to an art or science, to politics or profession.

When my university teachers talked of the liberation of work, they did not mean domestic help in rural New South Wales. I knew I was supposed to feel excitement and anticipation as they spoke the word "work," but all I could think of was standing at the bottom of that hill at the end of a long day, with heavy buckets of stinking slop hanging off my shoulders, wondering if I could make it up the hill.

In 2007, Natasha Stott-Despoja, writing in the *Age* on work and family, bemoaned the absence of equal numbers of men and women in politics, business and the law. She is right – it does matter that our elites include fewer women than men. Women are now investing time, money and energy as never before in training and education. Our society needs their talents. So what exactly is the problem?

A *Good Weekend* feature in 2002 depicted a woman lawyer conducting a 10 p.m. international phone conference. An unremarkable event, except that while making "pithy remarks" in a "steady voice," she was also on all fours, rocking back and forth in premature labour with her first child and suppressing moans of pain. She had "promised herself months earlier that having a baby would not compromise her career. During her pregnancy she had worked even longer hours than usual to prove her commitment to the job ... [She] didn't want to be the one who ended [the conference call] ... 'you'll look like a wuss.'"

Our society is hoping to get something of immense value – talented women working at a time of increasing labour shortages – for nothing. We are not doing even remotely enough to support them in combining child-rearing and work. Far more women, surveys show, want children than end up having them. Why? It is not just inadequate provision of affordable child-care or no paid maternity leave. The problem is far deeper. It lies with the values surrounding the ideal worker norm – like the woman above giving birth while conducting a phone conference, afraid of acknowledging her maternal self – and our reluctance to do the hard work of adapting to the needs of a new workforce. The old norms are based on the male life cycle: training early, getting established in the professions, working long hours, taking no time out and competing against other men. At one academic conference the young women attending were instructed to write several extra articles *before* motherhood, and to put them away in a drawer. After giving birth, they could then submit them at regular intervals, to conceal any gap children might create in their publication record! As Hochschild says, curriculum vitae in every profession are premised on a male or childless life pattern:

> Male-styled careers introduce women to a new form of time con-
> sciousness; it is not age measured against beauty ... but age
> measured against achievement ... Time is objectified in the aca-
> demic vita, which grows longer with each article and book, and not
> with each ... political meeting or child ... What is won for the
> [child]... is lost to the vita.

Career women, unlike career men, are far more likely to be childless. That is not just a matter of choice. It is one consequence of our bloody-minded recalcitrance when it comes to altering institutions to recognise women's distinctive life patterns. A woman's peak fertility period lies between her early twenties and early thirties. Given that we expect our highly educated young women to train for longer, into their mid-to-late twenties, and then get established in a profession, that leaves an extraordinarily short window of opportunity to have children. Not just child-birth, but the most intense years of child-rearing occur in the same period of peak career development. It is not so much a case of "have it all" as "do it all" and "at the same time"! We expect our talented and able young women to adapt to male-style institutions, not vice versa. One tragic consequence of this is women who would love to be mothers, but leave it too late. Over the last few years there has been an outpouring of women's grief over this issue, most notably raised by the journalist Virginia Haussegger.

Our outdated work practices, based on the long-hours culture of "pres-enteeism," need to be radically overhauled. Too many of our most valued professions have institutionalised extreme worker patterns resembling those of a corporate workaholic circa 1950. Short of a night nanny, a day nanny, and maybe a holiday nanny as well, a sixteen-hour day at a law office doesn't permit fathers, let alone mothers, to be effective workers as well as attentive parents.

It suits us to let mothers "manage like a man," like the woman in the *Good Weekend* article. It is in our self-interest to continue much as before the equal-opportunities revolution, wilfully blind to the extent of the change really needed. Men do not give birth, breast-feed, and only rarely have they been primary parents responsible for the everyday care of a child. Much of the furore over women breastfeeding in public is part Puritan-ism, part insistence that if women enter formerly male-only spaces, they should hide their female, especially maternal, embodiment. One pub-lisher told me that her boss, on encountering a mother breastfeeding a baby in her office, shouted furiously, "Breasts don't belong in the office!" But they do, of course, so long as they are sheathed beneath a silk blouse in a power suit, for male delectation, not lactation!

When a young, single business executive tells me she is afraid to take more than one week's holiday at a time lest she lose her job, then her firm has sent her a powerful message about the possibilities of combining work with future family life. When a talented young doctor gives up the hope of doing her preferred specialty and becomes a GP because the punishing work schedule means she would hardly see her children, then the extreme worker norm operates as a form of covert discrimination. Yet we claim airily, "Oh, it was her choice!" Our consciences are clear.

The dilemmas of the baby versus the briefcase, however, as important as they are, should not limit the scope of our understanding of the decisions women make around family and work. Almost all of those who make the running on work and family and their relative value come from the Churchillian upper class of workers. They are writers not racehorse strappers, lawyers not waitresses, professors not the carers who wipe children's bottoms at the child-care centre or feed elderly parents with a spoon in the nursing home. That point is especially pertinent in the light of deteriorating labour-market conditions for casual and low-skilled workers under policies like the late, unlamented WorkChoices.

Those writing the elite "better than sex" cultural script on work have jobs which are a source of honour, power, status and money. Work is so desirable for this group that it is addictive. Their identities are tied to work – one might say, they *are* their work – to such a degree that anyone stepping out of this world to care for children might rightly dread the question, "What do you do?" Ann Crittenden, a Pulitzer Prize nominee and former *New York Times* journalist, quit work after giving birth to her son. After she had been a stay-at-home mother for a while, someone stopped her in the street and asked, "Weren't you Ann Crittenden?"

I believe we should consider the needs of such women with the respect and seriousness their situation deserves. Nevertheless, it is not the whole of womanhood, by any means.

Mothers at the School Gate

> There's just a disappearance of mum at home in a suburban home living on a sort of average wage and walking to the corner every morning and taking the kids to the bus stop. She just isn't there.

She's working, or she's unemployed, or she's in a Volvo car with a very special life. But there are very few of those. – Pru Goward, Sex Discrimination Commissioner, November 2003

If my standpoint on the question of work altered along with the kind of work I did, it was motherhood which changed my views on the meaning of children.

From the late 1980s to 2006, every afternoon I drove to pick my children up from school. We live in the outer suburban fringe of Melbourne in a marginal seat, where elections are won or lost. Traffic is invariably a problem – you either arrive early or late if you want to avoid the crush. At the school car park there are so many parents – overwhelmingly mothers but also dads, grandmas and car-pooling friends – to greet the kids. It is situated among identikit neighbourhoods with schoolyards likewise thronging with parents.

For the most part, these are not homemakers. Most do work, although they were usually at home when children were small. Their work is part-time and shaped around the rhythms of children's lives. The older kids get, the longer the hours they work, often to pay for the educational needs of their children. They are stalwart volunteers: the fundraisers and lynch-pins of local community life. They run everything that matters in the world of the child: playgroups, fundraising for kindergarten committees, school canteens, local sporting clubs and cultural activities.

Their relations with each other are strong. I recently had dinner in a local restaurant with members of a women's group. One, a rambunctious local government councillor, was still mainly at home. With two teenagers, she thought it a crucial time to "be there." Recently she had a bad injury; all the mums from her original mother's group brought her cooked meals and cared for her. As I sat there, I thought of the new neo-liberal rhetoric of social "inclusion": you are excluded from anything valuable in a community unless you engage in paid work; we need to get women out of the rut of being economically "inactive" or "unemployed."

Outside the fast lane of the dilemmas of the dual-career couple that dominates discussion of work and family in our newspapers is a whole countryside of Australian families making different choices. They differ greatly from the work-centred group who write opinion columns and reports for the Human Rights and Equal Opportunity Commission, for whom the question "What do you do?" carries real emotional freight.

In contrast, among the forgotten women, as I came to call them, it could be years before anyone bothered to ask, "And what do you do?" They knew what you did! You were part of the invisible community, putting your shoulder to the wheel of parenthood. These women put the most extraordinary amount of time and effort into their children doing well in life. They are incredibly hard workers. Some of that work ethic is applied to paid work. But most of it is discharged in keeping kids safe, making sure they do things which develop their talents, give them a direction in life and keep them connected. Fathers are there too, and grandparents, as well as some paid caregivers. But by far the largest labour force raising children is maternal.

I tried a simple thought experiment. If these women changed their lives to the Get to Work program, working full time from the earliest weeks in their children's lives, would it make their lives better? It would be false to say that work meant nothing. Work certainly bestowed adult status, contributed some income over which they had autonomy, gave a welcome break from the kids. But for the mothers I met – who worked at the supermarket checkouts, the vegetable shops, the dry cleaners, ran their own car-cleaning service, the aged-care nurse working three days a fortnight – to work the 1950s male life pattern would have diminished their pleasure in life, not enhanced it. It would have done so because their chief pleasure in life was children.

Feminism gains its moral authority from being universal – on behalf of all women. It loses that moral power of suasion if it is revealed as acting mainly or exclusively on behalf of sectional interest groups, for example where a highly educated, high-earning elite group interprets and insists, on behalf of other women, what their interests might be.

My observations about the differences among women have a solid empirical base. The British sociologist of work Catherine Hakim has examined differences among women through hardhat empirical studies. During a ten-year stint working in the British Department of Employment as a labour-market analyst, Hakim noticed that the facts radically contradicted the "monolithic consensus," which held that women's work rates were climbing, that all women wanted to work, preferably full time, and that the only barrier to them doing so was the absence of child-care. Before that experience, Hakim, herself both childless and work-centred, accepted all the key tenets of the zeitgeist:

> We all believed it. It was completely taken for granted assumption
> that the only thing that held women back from the labour market
> was discrimination.

Hakim gives a telling example of these assumptions. When in the late 1990s the British Cabinet Office's Women's Unit organised a major research program called "Listening to Women," it found the diversity of preferences on work and family that is typical of all modern societies. While two-thirds of women felt that a job was the best way to independence for a woman, one-third thought women should not try to combine career and family. Those surveyed were evenly divided on whether a housewife's role was as rewarding as paid work. "Women were clear that the full-time mother role is undervalued by society" and that the pressure was now on women to return to work quickly. They wanted greater recognition and financial support for mothering. It was not the absence of child-care which kept full-time mothers out of the workforce, but rather the fact that "motherhood and parenting took a central place in their lives." In the absence of financial need, only 5 per cent of mothers preferred full-time work, three-quarters wanted a part-time job, and one-fifth wanted not to work at all.

Despite being commissioned by the Blair government, which prided itself on developing "evidence-based policies," the published summary of the research, deliciously entitled *Voices, Turning Listening into Action*, made no mention of diversity. Instead it emphasised education and training, access to paid work, job segregation, the pay gap, and child-care services for working mothers.

Hakim rejected the vanguardist temptation for an elite to decide, on behalf of other women, what constitutes the good life. "Difference and diversity are now the key features of the female population ... And in a civilised society difference and diversity are positively valued." Hakim argued that the answer to the age-old question, "What do women want?", was to be found in an extensive range of international data on women's preferences. Instead of elites imposing their own work-centred priorities on women, and promoting them as universal and natural, she argued that policy makers should ask them what their priorities are and "start taking them seriously when they tell us."

We live in what Hakim calls "a new scenario." That new scenario was ushered in by several transformations: the equal-opportunities revolution, which abolished the old legal framework that engineered the bread-winner/ homemaker family; the contraceptive revolution, which enabled women to control their own fertility; and economic changes, which meant many more part-time jobs became available. Lastly, there was a shift in the modern sensibility to individualism where there is "no fixed model for the good life."

The new scenario means modern women not only face genuine choices about how they will live their lives, but make very different ones. By pulling together a huge range of international empirical research, Hakim identified three broad preference groups among women. A minority of work-centred women, between 10 and 30 per cent (the larger or smaller estimate relates to how much state support is provided for this choice), prefer continuous full-time work throughout life. They are more likely to have fewer children or to be childless (and to be single). The polar opposite are home-centred women, also numbering between 10 and 30 per cent of all women. Their chief pleasure in life is children and family life. Such women have larger families and only work if they have to. The majority of modern women (around 70 per cent) are part of the third, largest and quite complex group, which Hakim calls "adaptive." Adaptive women adopt a compromise position, wanting the best of both worlds by combining family and work in different ways. "Sequential" mothers stay home while children are young, and increase work commitments as they get older. Others work part time throughout. Adaptive women can also become work-centred and career-oriented as their children become independent.

Hakim is not arguing that *only* preferences determine women's lives. A marriage ending; finding unexpected pleasure or frustration in motherhood; inflexible workplaces and the absence of child-care — all of these can shape whether or not preferences are fulfilled. A significant proportion of women *do* want a life very close to the old male career pattern. For the first time in human history, it is possible to realise such ambitions. What the evidence doesn't support, however, is the notion that a life where paid work is the central life activity is a *universal desire of all women*. In the new scenario, Hakim maintains, preferences become very important. Rather than seeing that as a problem, Hakim argues, in the liberal tradition of John Stuart Mill, that "according to the principles of modern society, *the question rests with women themselves — to be decided by their own experience, and by the use of their faculties*." How women are to live is up to the women themselves.

Women's diversity of preference on family and work is rarely acknowledged. Invariably newspaper and academic articles trumpeting revolutionary change, and supposedly showing women's newfound attachment to the labour force, rely on the dramatic surge in women's workforce *participation rates*. Hakim is especially scathing about relying on data that use employment measures as vague and imprecise as "more than one hour a week." Such statistics are crude, don't encompass the complexities of the new scenario and give a seriously misleading account of many women's priorities. They lump career women working eighty-hour weeks at Goldman Sachs together with mothers working a few hours weekly at Bi-Lo while Dad or Grandma minds the kids. Critical to Hakim's new analysis was the number of hours worked.

None of this is to deny the very real, even dramatic change among some mothers, especially those with high incomes, or with one child and a strong desire for a career. Angela Shanahan, writing in the Australian, pointed out the family-centred reality of women's work patterns:

> In October 2006 research published by the Australian Institute of Family Studies, only 38 per cent of mothers with a baby under one are employed at all and, of these, 43 per cent are part-timers working from one to 15 hours a week, while another 25 per cent work 16–24 hours. The most common occupational category of employed mothers with infants, at 30 per cent, is the professional. A few more mothers start to enter the workforce in their child's second year, but once again most work few hours. Not until children are almost school age are 60 per cent of their mothers employed, with 52 per cent of working mothers whose youngest child is in the four-to-five age group working fewer than 24 hours a week, half of those fewer than 16 hours.

Work patterns reflect opportunity cost and cultural values, as much as or more than "necessity." The pattern for professional women to return earlier is borne out overseas. Ann Crittenden shows that in the US "nationwide one-third of new mothers of annual income of $50,000 or more return to work after three months. They are less likely to stay home with a new baby than low-income mothers, only one-fourth of whom return to work."

Social class changes the standpoint on children. Deborah Keys, from the Key Centre for Women's Health in Society at Melbourne University, has done some striking new work on young homeless mothers. What comes across in her work, above all, is the sense of purpose in the young women's voices. Life is lived, for the first time, on behalf of another, and that is felt to be inspiring. Here's what one young mother says:

> Tyler's uplifting for me, encouraging. He's got a lot of impact on my life. He's changed the way I think about life in general. Gives me something to look forward to and wake up for the next morning – a reason to keep on going.

Similar judgments about motherhood are also made by poor women in the US. Kathryn Edin and Maria Kefalas interviewed poor mothers in Philadelphia. The mothers speak movingly of rising to the challenge of taking responsibility for a child, despite difficult circumstances: "It is a wonderful feeling because this is my child and he can come to me … his future is in my hands." Another says, "Your children have to come first" and "They didn't ask to be brought into this world, and it's up to you to take care of them and you gotta see to their needs."

These women say that motherhood changed their life. It gave them a reason and purpose larger than the self for getting out of bed in the morning. It is a *moral* turning point in their lives. In some cases, it provides the incentive to break away from destructive relationships with men. It is not a life *opposed* to achievement and work, either. In many cases, children provide the incentive to make a go of things at work.

Well-educated, affluent women don't necessarily agree with the Linda Hirshmans of the world either. In her book *Maternal Desire*, Daphne De Marneffe raised the not-insignificant matter of the *pleasure* women may take in caring for their child. She writes: "Feminism has not always helped me. How many times I have encountered a feminist book filled with innovative ideas for changed gender relations, the acceptance of whose argument requires just one small price: that I relinquish my attachment to spending time caring for my children." At that moment, she writes, "the author and I inhabit truly different emotional worlds. What seems like a rational, sane and human solution to her seems like a Faustian bargain to me."

In similar vein, Labor MP Tanya Plibersek, responding to Anne Summers' book *The End of Equality*, noted: "If you offered the average parent eighty hours free, top quality child-care a week, they wouldn't take it. There is an additional factor, which Summers touches on but does not explore adequately: we want time with our families."

On this question, Hakim cites an example as close to a perfect choice situation as you could get. In Finland in the first three years after the birth of a child, there is a choice of a home-care allowance and job-protected leave (that is, you can return to your previous job) or a free child-care place and early return to work. By the mid-'90s, about three-quarters of Finnish mothers used the home-care allowance instead of day-care. "Usage," writes Hakim, "is twice as high among mothers with low usual earnings as among higher paid women."

*

> I think the government's very conscious that there is no reversal in the trend to women going back to work with small children. The only thing stopping more women from going back to work with children is the shortage of child-care. —Pru Goward

Australian parents overall are cautious and judicious in their use of child-care. They are dubious about long day-care for babies and toddlers, and favour full-time mother care or part-time work. The older the child, the more parents think child-care is appropriate. The Get to Work program favoured by elites – full-time day-care and full-time work for mothers – is the path preferred by a minority of families in any country. Concern about early child-care and preference for home care is universal. In every country where information is collected, parental or mother care for the very young is preferred. Of course modern societies should provide high quality child-care places for those who want or need to use them. Australia needs more places than are presently provided. But to the extent we fund child-care to the exclusion of parental care, the trajectory of public policy will be in clear violation of the principles of a democratic state.

At present in Australian opinion polls, most parents regularly express the desire to care for their own small children. Australian opinion data collected in 2001 for the International Social Survey Program, a sophisticated periodic survey of a large representative national sample with carefully designed and tested questions, showed "a widespread preference" for mother care. Seventy-one per cent of Australian mothers surveyed thought women with children under six should stay home, 27 per cent thought they should work part time, and only 2 per cent believed they should work full time. When asked to rate their *personal* preferences on working or staying home with young children (a different approach to being asked about the ideal), more than 81 per cent of the women surveyed gave strong and warm responses to staying home. Only 9 per cent gave warm responses to the idea of full-time work. It is not simply traditionalism. Australians have a good opinion of working mothers. They "widely endorse the idea that maternal employment is, in general, a major contribution to the family." A clear majority agreed with the statement: "A working mother can establish just as warm and secure a relationship with her children as a mother who does not work." However, only 30 per cent thought it was okay for both parents to work full time when children were young. Not doing this was seen as a major financial sacrifice, but worth it.

Despite increases in women working, most Australian parents do not use long hours for child-care for babies and toddlers. Part-time care is preferred and utilised, rather than ten hours a day, five days a week. In 2005, for example, a mere 7 per cent of parents used formal child-care for infants under one. Around 31 per cent used it at age one. A little over 50 per cent by age three – and much of that was for part-time, pre-school-type activities. Only 38 per cent of four-year-olds went to formal child-care; as many went instead to pre-school. Of those children who used formal care, almost 50 per cent used it for less than ten hours per week.

The largest group of those using child-care did so for one day per week. Only 7 per cent used it for more than thirty-five hours a week.

When Pru Goward claims that "the only thing stopping more women from going back to work with children is the shortage of child-care," where is the evidence? Sixty-three per cent of all parents said they did not want child-care because they preferred to care for children themselves. Only 6 per cent of families needed more child-care. Of that 6 per cent, only one-third could not find places. It was the same proportion, the ABS statisticians note, in 1999, 2002 and 2005.

What women want, then, is clear. What about children, though?

The Melbourne psychotherapist Frances Salo-Thompson once made a simple but profound point to me about child-rearing. The most important thing, she said, is that a child feels *enjoyed*. As I listened, a memory flashed out from years back. I was teaching at Melbourne University and scurrying to a class. In the staff common room, I saw out of the corner of my eye a mother holding a baby aloft in the air, glorying in her presence. They were both gazing into one another's eyes and laughing. There was aliveness and intensity but also an easy playfulness in the mother's face, mirrored back to her by the joyous baby.

In the last decade and a half there has been an explosion of new knowledge about what makes children flourish or flounder, embark on life pathways which are either hopeful or ominous. The early-childhood story is an ecumenical one; we must take seriously the circumstances of *all* children, whether in relation to maternal depression, poor quality child-care, in circumstances of affluence and poverty.

One of the best books summarising for the layperson this rich new seam of knowledge is *Why Love Matters* by the British psychotherapist Sue Gerhardt. It is a little-known fact that in the long-running and most sophisticated study to date of child-care, done by the US National Institute of Child Health and Human Development (NICHD), the most significant finding was that it is parents, for good or ill, who have most effect on how a child turns out. That is true even when the child is in child-care. The science shows the ingredients of a healthy childhood are very consistent, says Dr Jack Shonkoff, author of *From Neurons to Neighbourhoods*: "The most important magic ingredient is the quality and the stability of the relationships that children have with the adults in their lives."

The first important element is a baby forming a secure attachment to their parents. It is a kind of falling in love. It is the most important task of the first year. Emphasising that a baby's sense of self can only come into being within a relationship, the British psychotherapist Donald Winnicott said, "There is no such thing as a baby; there is a baby and someone." Human infants are aware of and primed for social relatedness from the earliest moments.

Most mothers – around three-quarters in a non-risk sample – will form a secure attachment with their child. A secure attachment is aided by parents being promptly and emotionally responsive to a baby, sensitively reading their particular infant's needs, which can seem so chaotic and hard to understand at first, but which gradually, hour by hour, day by day, slowly settle into predictable patterns. A secure baby is confident that their needs – comfort, contact, hunger, thirst and pain – will be met. They can turn to a loved adult who will respond and help. Their expectations of others are benign; the world is a safe and trustworthy place.

But consider another baby, left wet, cold or lying in a dirty nappy, left hungry or screaming for long periods. No one comes or only comes in unpredictable ways. Or is harsh, angry and rejecting when they do arrive. That baby's feelings are more likely to be panicky, and angry. Later, as a child and adult, they are more likely to be hyper-alert and hyper-vigilant. They have no confidence their needs will be met.

A human infant is the "least neurologically developed of all primates" and adds 70 per cent of its structure after birth. That makes us, as Lauren Porter of the New Zealand Centre of Attachment explains, "unavoidably interdependent as a species." It also explains why large differences in environments can change the brain. There are neurobiological consequences of being loved or neglected. Nurture affects hidden bodily regulatory systems in the infant – temperature, blood sugar, stress hormones like cortisol and even growth hormones. Child-trauma specialist Bruce Perry shows a photo of a severely neglected three-year-old child whose brain is both different and markedly smaller than a child from a normal family.

Children judged secure as infants have many advantages later in childhood. Two-year-olds assessed as secure were enthusiastic and persistent in solving tasks, showed more joyousness and were more able to follow instructions, less likely to collapse in frustration. They were more likely to express positive emotions such as delight, to smile, laugh and share pleasurable feelings. Insecure kids, by contrast, confronted with the same task, became anxious and whiny, collapsing under pressure. As pre-schoolers, secure children were more flexible, curious and socially competent. They were more assertive about what they wanted, and more likely to be leaders. They had higher levels of self-esteem and ego resilience.

They were also more independent. This last finding on independence is important, because there is a lot of confusion about what makes for an independent child. Some think it is about toughening them up early by leaving them to cry for long periods. Yet psychologists have found that children whose dependency needs as babies were accepted and responded to promptly and sensitively were the ones who later became the most independent children.

Secure children were more empathetic. One psychologist remarked: "It's no good trying to tell and admonish a child to be empathetic, you get an empathetic child by being empathetic with the child. The child's understanding of relationships can only be from the relationships he's experienced." By middle childhood and adolescence, kids with early secure attachments made friends more easily. In contrast, insecure children were more likely to be bullies or bullied. Insecure boys in whom aggression was "particularly marked" were, according to the same psychologist, more likely to "bully, lie, cheat, destroy things, brag, act cruelly, disrupt the class, swear, threaten, argue, throw temper tantrums, become defiant. Alternately, they were more prone to be shy, apathetic, and withdrawn."

Another important aspect of the early years is attunement between caregiver and child. When infant researcher Daniel Stern slowed down videos of mothers engaging in babbling and cooing, playing peek-a-boo or tickling, he realised that an amazing conversation was going on. He called it the mother–baby dance. Within these non-verbal exchanges there was reciprocal turn-taking. The communications had their own rhythm, beat, precision and even a crescendo. By sharing a baby's feeling of excitement, for example, the mother amplified and extended the pleasure. Stern commented, "What is at stake here is nothing less than the shape of and extent of the shareable inner universe."

Such finely tuned, exquisite responsiveness can be seen even more vividly in an experiment done by Edward Tronick. When he asked mothers to mimic the still, blank and unresponsive face of a depressed person, babies responded by looking alarmed, trying to gain their mother's attention, almost throwing themselves out of their seat in an attempt to re-animate her. Finally they crumpled and withdrew, wailing, pitiful to behold.

Attachment and attunement in the first few years help the developing child to build up what psychologists call an internal working model. As the psychologist Ron Lally says, it's as if a child is putting spectacles on in the early years through which they view the world forever after, an emotional map of the world. When things have gone well, a child will move forward in life with optimism and trust. But if their background has been very troubled, they are more likely to assume the world is malign. An abused child, for example, may flinch when a caring teacher raises their hand, or expect rejection from friends and future partners. In contrast, secure attachments help a child to face the world with a more trusting and hopeful outlook, to form affectionate and trusting relationships with friends and later partners. There are intergenerational consequences. There is good evidence that patterns of attachment, to a considerable degree, are reproduced by the next generation.

The final and crucial aspect of healthy development shaped in the early years is the capacity for emotional regulation. How we manage, process, reflect on and thus control our emotions is critical for our relations with others, in the family, school and workplace. When unregulated impulses like rage or fear surge up and threaten to overwhelm us, the neo-frontal cortex – our social brain – says, "Calm down, wait a minute." Is it wise to hit my teacher or schoolmate who just made that criticism? And so on.

Babies are not born with the ability to regulate their emotions. It comes from being cared for by responsive caregivers who help them to regulate their internal states. The younger the baby, the less capacity they have for enduring negative feelings, waiting or coping. By being soothed and cared for on countless occasions, children gradually take over these vital functions and can cope with emotions by themselves, calming and soothing themselves. It doesn't happen overnight. But it does happen, bit by bit, little piece by little piece, as the early years unfold. Emotional regulation is one of the keys to good emotional health.

Parents can be daunted by a sense of the importance of the early years. Yet many simple, everyday acts promote good infant mental health. We know breastfeeding provides the best nutrition. It gives equally important *emotional* sustenance. There is skin-on-skin contact. The warmth of touch stimulates other neural pathways. On the left side a baby hears their mother's heartbeat, as they heard it in the womb, at a steady rhythm which soothes. At the breast they are just the right distance to focus on mother's face. Positive eye contact, neurobiologists explain, is incredibly important. Smiling at a baby, for example, releases natural opiates in their brain. A loving gaze stimulates the hormones which help the brain to grow.

Take another simple act: a father reading to a child. A warm touch, bodily contact, gives a feeling of security. A soothing, comforting voice, the richness of language in the story, the act of imagining the story, and the closeness of the relationship, add to the association of emotional security and pleasure with learning and reading, warmth as well as stimulation and interest.

Extreme neglect – like the famous case of the Romanian orphanages where a child is rarely touched, talked to or soothed – can result in profound changes to the brain. It may be very hard ever to make up for that later on – however loving the family. If children grow up under chronic stress, they have higher levels of stress hormones in their system. In turn, that may lead later to high levels of reactivity – the underlying neurochemistry of the brain has been altered to deal with a pervasive sense of threat. The child's anger and anxiety switch is flicked permanently on high. In extreme cases, if a child is neglected and abused, permanent changes may occur in the brain, the result of which may be aggression and depression. "A feeling state can become a trait. The child becomes hyper-alert … ready to flip on the least provocation." If no deep attachments are formed to other human beings, empathy, the capacity to feel or identify with another's pain, just doesn't develop.

The new research can easily be misrepresented. It can be distorted by conservatives to prove that "every mother must stay at home," conveniently overlooking where parenting is abusive or the facts about the consequences of maternal depression. On the other hand, it can be conscripted by an alliance of ideological feminism and the billion-dollar child-care industry to imply that "every child must be placed in the hands of the child-care professionals." Both readings are terrible distortions. It is the latter, however, which has become the central interpretation of the early-childhood story in the elite cultural script.

The "farewell to maternalism" has been accompanied by a new ideology of childhood. As deeply as Western elites have become disenchanted with maternalism, they have become enchanted with a new ideal – early child-care. Two substitute ideals emerged from the women's movement. The first was the genuinely radical break with the child-rearing past, an ideal of shared parental care. The second was what Joan Williams calls the "full-commodification" solution – institutional child-care. It is the second, rather than the first, which has succeeded beyond all expectations.

The reason lies less with its merits and more with its adaptability to the market. It is not a high quality, not-for-profit community sector, the dream of the early feminists, that is the fastest growing segment in child-care. It is the international for-profit corporate providers, such as ABC Learning. Yet if child-care is now a billion-dollar business, again we strike a strange paradox. It has been left-leaning progressives who have disenchanted us with mother care and enchanted us with the wonders of child-care, legitimising the commercialisation of child-rearing.

There has developed a powerful international movement to rationalise and standardise childhood. It is preoccupied not only with freeing women to work, but with weeding the child-rearing garden of unfit parents. The ambition goes way beyond what most Australians, including me, would support: the provision of high quality care for those who want or need it, or the provision of intervention projects for at-risk kids. Child-rearing, in this vision, is all the better for being rationalised, done by trained professionals and supervised by a centralised bureaucracy. The vagaries of untrained and uncertified parents are to be replaced from birth to five by the child-care centre, which will be the panacea, the cure-all for every modern problem on the landscape – poverty, welfare dependency, delinquency and crime.

The early-childhood story above does not tell us that only mothers can care for children. It tells us that *love* is important, rather than precisely who provides it. Yet it is also true that given the realities of the modern labour market, with low-paid, often untrained child-care workers struggling with high ratios of children to staff, child-care of the quality needed is all too rare. Those crucial elements of responsive, sensitive care, which fosters secure attachment, attunement and emotional regulation, are going to be exceptionally difficult to produce on anything like a mass basis. Sue Gerhardt says:

> It's a very contentious area, but from my point of view babies need one to one attention. They need to be with people who really know them well, notice how they are and respond quickly to them. Now that I don't think is terribly likely to happen in a [day-care] situation. I don't think nurseries [child-care centres] are great for babies, and we do know that full-time care in nurseries has some quite bad effects on children who go into that system.

In Australia, despite a regulatory system and notwithstanding some excellent and dedicated providers, as a whole we do not have the quality needed. Pam Cahir of Early Childhood Australia says, "It's rubbish to say we have quality child-care in Australia." Cahir points to large child/carer ratios, large staff-turnover and poor pay and conditions as major factors undermining quality. Cahir described our child-care regulations, which allow one caregiver for five babies, as a disgrace:

> If you have two adults, often young and untrained, each caring for five babies, that means when one baby is being fed and held, the other is caring for nine babies. Infants can't be comforted, crying infants can't be picked up. These carers are barely able to change and feed the babies, let alone have time to play with them and give them the stimulation and affection they need.

Child-care workers are leaving the industry in droves, says Cahir, because the job is just too hard.

That children may be stressed under such circumstances is shown by recent findings on cortisol in child-care children. Cortisol is a potent stress hormone. Normally cortisol levels in children are highest in the morning and lowest in the afternoon. Since the late '90s, researchers have discovered that a full day in centre-based care, compared with being at home with parents or in home-based child-care settings, can be associated with a significant increase in cortisol levels in the second half of the day. Secure attachments, as well as "touching, holding and responsive care in the early years," promote an individual's ability to manage stress in later life. By contrast:

> Stress in infancy is particularly damaging, as high levels of cortisol impact on the development of a range of neurotransmitters … whose pathways in the brain are still being built. The outcome of this is long-term difficulties in self and emotional regulation.

So what might stress an infant?

> Stress is created when the individual is threatened or feels insecure
> or uncertain … Separation from the attachment figure is one of the
> key stressful events in early childhood. Children who attend child-
> care routinely experience stress through separation and research
> has commonly identified these children as "at risk" for negative
> long-term outcomes. Children in child-care are found to have ele-
> vated cortisol compared to children in the home environment.

In the long term this has the potential to create in adults "heightened fear-fulness and greater vulnerability to stressors."

The researchers Margaret Sims, Andrew Guilfoyle and Trevor Parry studied children in the toddler through pre-school age group, in Australian child-care centres. The majority were in non-profit community centres: "no corporate centre approached agreed to participate, and few private centres did so." Even in centres considered "satisfactory" by accreditation bodies, children showed elevated cortisol. Only at the highest level of care quality did children's cortisol levels show the normal pattern.

One recent British study found that 90 per cent of babies experienced a dramatic jump in cortisol levels when placed even in high quality day-care. The cortisol levels of separated babies doubled compared with being at home. Even after months of adaptation, cortisol levels declined slightly, but remained higher in the child-care setting than at home. One 2003 US study found the effect was particularly strong in the toddler age group. Other studies have found it is also present, though less strongly, in ages three to four. The children were in medium to very high quality centres. The lower the quality the stronger the finding, but higher cortisol was also clearly still present in centres judged by careful measures to be excellent. The centres studied had one caregiver to two or three infants, far better than what Australian child-care regulations allow.

Higher cortisol, researchers suggest, may "have contributed to the negative outcomes associated with child-care attendance."

What kind of negative outcomes?

Since the late 1980s, a steady stream of evidence has linked extensive hours of infancy in child-care with increased aggression – a "more anxious and angry child." This evidence does not apply to three- and four-year-old children of pre-school age, but to infants and toddlers. In 1990 the prestigious US National Institute of Child Health and Human Development set up a longitudinal study to examine the effects of child-care. It carefully took account of care quality, age of entry, number of hours as well as parental characteristics. One of the most comprehensive and sophisticated studies of child-care ever undertaken, it involves more than 1100 children from ten US cities.

The study consistently found high quality care to have advantages for children over poorer quality care. There were cognitive advantages to child-care as opposed to home care, although these were modest and faded over time. Working mothers could take heart, too, from the finding that by itself maternal employment did not increase insecurity of attachment. Insecurity increased only when combined with other factors: when mothers were low on "sensitivity" and the child-care was for more than ten hours a week, or of relatively poor quality, or was unstable.

There were several problems, however, which showed up despite high quality care. Longer hours in child-care negatively affected mother–infant sensitivity and attunement. "More time in care predicts less harmonious mother–infant interaction and less sensitive mothering at 6, 15, 24 and 36 months of age, even when quality of child-care and family selection variables are controlled." When the study children were assessed at age four-and-a-half, those children who had experienced over thirty hours of care per week were three times more likely to show aggressive behavioural problems than children who had been in care for less than ten hours per week (17 compared with 6 per cent).

All relevant variables, including stability, quality and type of care, and parent attributes, were carefully taken into account. Quantity, not quality, was the issue. There was a straightforward linear, dose-for-dose relationship: the more time in care, the higher the aggressive-behaviour problems, such as "getting into many fights, showing cruelty, bullying or meanness to others, physically attacking other people, and being explosive, showing unpredictable behaviour." Children who had experienced longer hours of centre-based care continued to show more social and behavioural problems through the primary grades.

It is important not to catastrophise. Such results do not apply to every child in child-care. Not every study has made similar findings. In Australia, results have been mixed. University of Melbourne academic Kay Margetts also found that "more extensive non-parental care in the years closest to birth increases the risk of children having difficulty adjusting to the first year of schooling in all domains: social, behavioural and academic." The Longitudinal Study of Australian Children (LGSAC), by contrast, made the unusual finding that at age two to three, longer hours in centre care were associated with improved behavioural outcomes. Neither study, however, used a methodology as sophisticated or as thorough as the NICHD group.

When Edward Melhuish, an internationally respected British scholar on child-care, reviewed all the international child-care research for the British National Audit Office, he found other studies, even in Scandinavia, where quality is widely regarded as the best in the world, confirming the Anglo–American research.

One further decisive contribution to the debate was the results from two large, longitudinal British studies, one from Oxford University, another from London University, which again raised concerns about group care for the under-twos, while also giving favourable results for educational pre-school programs for children over three. The University of London concluded that: "high levels of group care before the ages of three (and particularly before the age of two) were associated with higher levels of antisocial behaviour at age three." Higher quality care reduced "antisocial/worried behaviour," but did not eliminate it.

Evidence of risks associated with longer hours of child-care has continued to gather. The NICHD study group, after reviewing other recent studies, concluded that "the timing and/or amount of early child-care have repeatedly, though not always, been related to problem behaviour in the early school years."

Two more large-scale studies, one in Canada and one from Stanford University, also reported negative emotional and behavioural problems associated with child-care. The Stanford study, of more than 14,000 children, found longer hours of child-care detrimental, especially for the under-twos:

> Not only do the negative behavioural effects appear for those with at least 15 hours of care per week, but additional care, as measured by at least 30 hours of center care, more than doubles this negative effect.

The earlier the centre-care attendance started, the more problems were found:

> the negative behavioral effects associated with center attendance, compared with parental care at home, are much greater for those who enter a center when younger than two years of age, and are particularly large for those who start at less than one year of age. For both low and high income children, starting a center program before the age of two is not particularly beneficial for cognitive development and appears to be detrimental for social development.

*

Despite such findings, we repeatedly see unqualified claims of the following kind from both political parties and governmental agencies in Australia:

> Quality child-care in the "early years" is also considered to be beneficial to a child through providing a stimulating, educational and

caring environment that aids a child's social, educational and physical development. Studies have shown that quality early-childhood programs serve as an early intervention device, aiding in reducing future social problems such as crime, unemployment and teenage pregnancies.

Based on such claims, both the Labor and Liberal parties entered into a bidding war over child-care during the recent election. How is such a mismatch between science and public policy possible? Here is how it's done.

According to the child-care lobby, for every $1 invested in child-care, there is a $7 return in terms of prevention of crime, delinquency and early school-leaving patterns. Many Australian government agencies and both major political parties have swallowed this "fact" hook, line and sinker. Don Edgar, the former director of the Australian Institute of Family Studies, claims that:

> Long-term studies show that for every dollar invested in quality child-care, we reap $7 saved in rates of later school failure, unemployment, crime and family breakdown ... Every hour spent in every form of child-care is a learning experience.

The illusion depends upon no one inquiring too deeply into the real facts of the matter. Let's take that much-quoted figure of $1 invested, $7 returned. Where does it come from?

It comes from the Perry Pre-school, which was a small-scale, targeted, high quality intervention project in the 1960s. It offered twelve hours a week of care to impoverished, profoundly disadvantaged African-American children. They were from troubled family backgrounds and developmentally delayed. It was a program not for infants, but for three- and four-year-olds. It was not ordinary day-care, but was a high quality intervention provided by genuine specialists with a home-visiting program to improve seriously inadequate parenting skills.

In 2006, a landmark British study, from the well-regarded London University EPPI Centre, debunked claims that for $1 invested in child-care, there will be a $7 return. Its focus is explicitly on the false application of Perry Pre-school–type data:

> The cost-benefit figures of seven or eight dollars saved for every one dollar spent are widely cited in the academic and popular press in many countries, and have frequently been cited by senior politicians in the UK … the widespread, international use of the most favourable headline findings, and in particular of the Perry High/Scope study, is unjustified … The targeting of low-income African-American children in ghettoised neighbourhoods, in a period of considerable racial tension, leads to considerable doubts about the generalisability of these interventions outside their original context.

James Heckman, an advocate for targeted interventions, is dismayed at the distortion of his message. Writing in the *Wall Street Journal*, Heckman says: "Science doesn't support universality … We have to promote [early-childhood programs] more cautiously."

Jennifer Buckingham, in her review of the research for the Centre for Independent Studies, notes that while Australian early-childhood academics routinely claim that a four-decade-old study of at-risk kids adapts with perfect felicity to Australia, the same researchers have also argued that any negative evidence from overseas does not apply here!

Such claims cannot be given credence when the fastest growing provider in the Australian market, ABC Learning, has just entered the US market with great success. Much Australian child-care is, sadly, increasingly similar to that provided by US for-profit corporate chains such as Kindercare Inc. Ironically, the corporate child-care chains have most benefited from the tireless work of legitimation that left progressives have performed in convincing gullible policy makers of the universality of the $7 for $1 figure. They have laughed all the way to the bank.

Buckingham lists seven identikit statements from key Australian government agencies along the lines of the oft-quoted figure. How is such unanimity produced? Few of those in the government agencies she quotes really know the evidence. They are overworked and time-pressed. That means they rely on the interpretation given by the "knowledge experts," the early-childhood professionals.

The professional "experts," however, are not necessarily disinterested white-coated scientists with a test tube in one hand and a lab report in the other. Even in the NICHD study group, twenty-two of the twenty-seven researchers were women whose professional lives were supported by child-care. One of their number, Alison Clarke-Stewart, even admitted to a journalist that she hoped to find a particular result: "I wanted to find out that child-care was good. I'm a working mother, but that's not the only reason. It made common sense to me."

Research evidence that arrives on policy makers' desks is filtered and edited. They read short, carefully selected summaries. In a fascinating paper, the Canadian academic and child-care activist Rianne Mahon is completely candid about the politicisation of the process. There is an international network of activists determined to install the early child-care agenda. Their strength, Mahon notes, comes from developing an international network of like-minded proponents, which "blurred the boundary" between "experts" and "transnational advocacy networks." In other words, child-care activists are also the "experts."

Mahon writes: "the end of maternalism" is "not simply the spontaneous response to a set of common challenges." Rather, it is occurring through a process of policy "learning" and "prescription" of a "particular flavour." She cites the OECD, and the Early Childhood Educational and Care Unit within it, as an especially important conduit for installing the child-care agenda. The OECD's role in propagating such ideas involves the "fast-tracking" of "expert" knowledge through member states. It involves the development and circulation of advice that is "essentialised," carefully selected, and "edited." The editing is most pronounced in the executive summaries, introductions and conclusions that are "most likely to be read by time-pressed policy makers." Like the Perry Pre-school data.

According to Mahon, through this process OECD nations are persuaded to "unlearn" ideas deemed incompatible with flexible labour markets and the needs of the new capitalism – like maternalism – and "learn" new ones, like the early child-care agenda. As one text put it, "such editing" "*helps to define economic and social reality,*" not just put into "words what already exists." "What is transmitted," summarises Mahon, is not simply research results "*but the very definition of common problems and prescribed solutions.*"

Here's an example in the Australian context. Overseas cortisol research shows kids in child-care are more likely to have elevated stress levels than those in parental care. The Australian researcher and child-care partisan Margaret Sims does research into cortisol in child-care – but only compares kids in higher quality and poorer quality child-care! Thus a crucial piece of information – that stress levels are usually less in parental care – is "edited" out. Translated into policy terms, that means we all cheer loudly for increased child-care funding at election time, without noticing that the parental-leave policies which have supported Northern European women in combining family and work don't even rate a mention.

Politically canny, the lobbyists know that politicians and the business community are especially responsive to the economic arguments. Businessman Charlie Coffey, for example, addressing a World Bank symposium on early child-care, quotes the famous figure: for every $1 invested in child-care, there is a $7 return. He does not mention the substantive literature on the associated risks. He quotes John Kenneth Galbraith: "The views of one articulate and affluent banker, businessman, lawyer, or acolyte economist are the equal of several thousand welfare mothers in the corridors of political power." Quite so.

Coffey then borrows the charming theme of the "trillium flower with its three petals," from Cornell University's "Linking Economic Development and Child Care Research Project." He quickly drops this natural poesy, however, and begins talking in the cool, hardheaded language of rational economics. The research:

> has demonstrated the economic importance of early care and education. Together the three petals capture the short and long-term economic contributions made by early-childhood services. One petal represents children and the investments in human development and education. Another represents the Regional Economy, investments in child-care as an industry that produces jobs and stimulates the economy. The third petal represents parents and the economic contributions they make to the economy, as employees and consumers. The economic contributions of children are considered long-term, because the pay-off largely occurs after the child matures.

The word "economic" appears four times in this paragraph, the word "economy" appears thrice, and the language of economics – investments and pay-offs – is everywhere. The word "love" appears nowhere. Rather, parents are re-defined as "employees and consumers." Even children are considered as human investment units, where the "pay-off" occurs in adulthood. This is the new vision.

Ironically, then, left progressives have inadvertently provided the new economic order with the rationale it needs to transform care into a commodity relation. Intimate human relations are redefined as care. Love is an anti-commodity relationship. Love cannot be reproduced, but caring can. It is exchangeable, reproducible, replaceable and able to be done for money. What the left progressives didn't count on, however, is that if all care can be transformed into a commodity relation, then it can also be transferred to the marketplace. Child-care is increasingly delivered not by the small, parent-friendly co-operatives envisaged by early feminists, but in huge international corporate child-care chains like ABC Learning Centres.

Yet there is another path. As Edward Melhuish observed, unless you compromise on quality, the cost of subsidising child-care for the under-twos is broadly comparable to generous parental leave. He points to the case of Sweden as evidence of what parents might want if they had a real choice:

> The Swedish case is very revealing – there was high quality infant care available to all and heavily subsidised. It was widely used in the '70s and '80s, but in the early '90s, parental leave was increased and now there is remarkably little use of child-care under 18 months. Parents voted with their feet.

LOVE'S LABOUR

Some goddesses devise a competition among nations, a kind of Olympics with a twist. Health and prosperity for all will be the prize granted to the nation that can collectively run the greatest distance in the shortest time. But only the goddesses know how long the race will last.

The first nation divides caring and running according to gender. Men run on ahead hard and fast in exchange for being in charge, while women come along behind them, looking after children, the sick and the elderly, as well as those injured in the race. They give birth to new runners to replace those exhausted. At first all goes well. Over time, however, women began to see the rewards given to the men for running far outweigh those bestowed on the carers. They know that many among them could run just as hard and fast as the men, and they demand equal rights. When the men resist, the women go out on strike, causing chaos. This nation is about to lose.

The second nation sees the pitfalls of excluding women from the race. It assumes the race will not last long and sets its members to compete "every person for themselves." Some citizens at first speed quickly away, but as the race goes on and on, many begin to fall by the wayside. There are few non-competitors left to care for the sick and the injured. Female runners have no time to give birth, or to care for children to replace ageing runners. Fertility drops sharply, and this nation can no longer reproduce itself. Before long it becomes clear that this nation, too, will lose the race.

All eyes turn to the third nation. Like the canny tortoise against the hare, it is making slow but steady progress. Everyone is required both to run and to take care of those who cannot run. Care is as valued as running. The strategy is less efficient in the short term, but as the long race wears on, it is revealed to have great strengths. While the first two nations by now have collapsed, the citizens from the third nation grow strong as well as fast, while "their freedom and equality foster ... their solidarity."

Nancy Folbre, the author of this parable, ends mischievously: "Of course they won the race. What did you expect? It was a race that goddesses designed."

In this story, the first society is the older traditional world which we are leaving behind, where a mixture of custom and patriarchal law meant the costs of care were borne exclusively by women. The second is a description of contemporary neo-liberal societies – where in Australia we are headed. Based on radical individualism and the values of the market-place, such societies treat adult life as if it is based solely on competitive achievement, rewarding achievement and penalising care. In them, women find themselves confronted with often insoluble dilemmas over work and care. The alternative society, where care and work are both shared and valued, is only half born.

In *The Commercialisation of Intimate Life*, Arlie Hochschild raises a central issue of our time: "Are we okay with the fact that baby may say his first word to the child-care worker, and grandma her last word to the nursing home aide?" She writes, too, of the devaluation of care. A 65-year-old man she interviewed, who cares for his elderly mother, says: "If a man is caring for others, calling, shopping, visiting, it shows the world he has failed as a man." Failed as a man?, Hochschild asked. He answers, "Yes, he *really has* failed as a man." Hochschild says, "Care: we haven't worked it through yet."

The Get to Work program favoured by our government and elite opinion does not do justice to the decisions that so many women make on a day-to-day basis on the question of care, whether they are in paid work or not. Nor does it do justice to the dependents for whom they are responsible. All societies need altruism, Folbre reminds us, a capacity to give and reward the work of care. *Pace* Linda Hirshman, there is another way of seeing the lives of women who shape their lives around care: not as leading "lesser lives," but as worthy of respect. Here is what Madeleine Bunting, a *Guardian* columnist, says of the way British mothers are spoken about:

Not cutting it – that's pretty much the gist … This was the refrain of the Women and Work Commission last week; it reminded me of a summit on women's productivity at No 11 just over a year ago. Women had to get into better jobs and work harder, a selection of highly productive women and Gordon Brown declared. You could hear the lashing of whips from these well-meaning slave drivers. But the whole debate about women's place in work is lopsided. They are not failures but astonishing successes … mothers' productivity is staggeringly high: the Office for National Statistics did a valuation of women's homemaking and care, and came up with a figure of £929bn, or 104 per cent of GDP. Combine that with the value of women's paid work, and they are easily outperforming the shockingly low productivity of men.

*

In October 2007 the former Families and Community Services minister, Mal Brough, addressed a forum organised by the Association for Children with a Disability. After listening to a harrowing and moving account from a woman who cared for her husband and two children with serious disabilities, Mr Brough put his foot in it. He said he was sympathetic to those people who "choose to do what you do." He attempted to correct himself but was angrily jeered by the audience. One member of the crowd yelled out, "We don't choose, we have to."

Rather than depicting care as the problem, or assuming that women can go on effortlessly delivering such care while also increasing their workforce participation, let's begin from a different standpoint. Folbre puts it like this:

> Today patriarchal coercion is unacceptable. On the other hand, pure selfish individualism is both ugly and unviable. Without at least some altruism, we cannot reproduce ourselves. If we believe we

have obligations to care for one another, we should decide what these are and how they should be enforced.

Eva Kittay, philosopher and mother of a profoundly disabled child, is a representative of a new type of feminism, which reminds us of what is left out when society is supposed to be an association of equals. It masks dependencies and asymmetries that form an inevitable part of the human condition. Humans are born vulnerable, and they die vulnerable. We may be born or become disabled, contract multiple sclerosis or cancer, become mentally ill, and grow old and frail. All of the natural and irrevocable parts of the human condition will need care. Some is temporary, like the care of children from whom adult caretakers can justly expect later reciprocity. Love's labour will and must always includes those among us who can never reciprocate, like the disabled or the chronically mentally ill. No just society will forget them. Nor can it ignore looking after those who dedicate their lives to care.

These feminists concentrate on the terrain of social reproduction and caregiving without which no market work could occur. They are looking for an alternative both to the unfairness of traditional patriarchal society, which assigned women to caregiving whatever their talents and preferences, but also to the individualist "dog eat dog" world of each person for themselves, and care on the cheap, which increasingly characterises modern society. Folbre points out Adam Smith's blind spot in his seminal work *The Wealth Of Nations*. Smith invokes self-interest as the lubricant of the marketplace, from "the butcher, or the brewer, or the baker that we expect our dinner." But who actually prepares that dinner and puts it on the table?

Wives and mothers. In Smith's world, were women, too, to act from self-interest? God forbid! "Self-interest was appropriate only to the impersonal world of the market."

The invisible hand of the market is dependent on the shadow economy of care. It is that which sets male breadwinners free to pursue their self-interest in market production and paid work, supposedly for the greater good of all.

Both neo-liberalism and Hirshman-style feminism share a flaw. They are based on the model of the self-interested rational individual, *homo economicus*. Yet applied to the relational world, *homo economicus* would be a self-interested, affectionless, ruthless psychopath. No viable family life or solution to the problems of care can be found here.

Many of the Get to Work commentators, who exhort women to do more paid labour, seem to assume that this caring work will go on pretty much as it always has even when women suffer a care penalty. In neo-liberal societies, in particular, we are hoping that we can go on free-riding on female care, reluctant to do much beyond providing cheap for-profit market alternatives to love's labour. We are loath to integrate dependency work into our economic system, for example by re-organising the labour market to acknowledge the fact that the new group of workers has obligations to vulnerable others. That leaves us with a monumental hole in our care budget – or, if you like, a care deficit.

While alternatives to family care, including commercialised care, will undoubtedly play an important part in the new scenario, it can never be the whole solution. Commercialising care cannot always ensure loving attentiveness, which is embedded in particularity and a shared history. Turning care over to the market – commodifying it – has inherent problems. To begin with, all the assumptions about the well-informed purchaser who can withdraw patronage from inadequate services fall down in the case of caregiving services. If people don't thrive in care, it can be difficult to find an alternative. Care services may be in such short supply, or so expensive, that the purchaser settles out of panic on the first, rather poor option they can find. Since services are always labour-intensive, any attempt to lift the quality of care raises the cost. There are limits to efficiency; care services cannot be standardised or depersonalised without great harm to the person cared for. Then there's what one might call the "moral hazard" of the commodification solution, as described by Folbre:

> Even if the actual decision-makers have the most exalted motives and
> want nothing but the best for those dependent on their choices … it
> is difficult for them to judge the quality of the ensuing care. After
> all, they are not the ones receiving it … in the face-to-face provision
> of care services with an emotional content, the quality of interaction
> can vary enormously. And this quality is difficult to assess.

The "full-commodification" model is flawed for other reasons, too.
Only the affluent will be able to afford good quality care. Moreover, commercialising child-care does nothing to alter ideal worker norms. These
rigid workplace norms mean that professional women must rely on poorer
women to do the care work. For, as globalisation finds a market for wom-
en's labour, so too does it produce poor women washed up on the shores
of globalisation who are then utilised to balance the care budget.

The fates of rich and poor women have drawn radically apart in the
new capitalism. In her 2004 essay "How Serfdom Saved the Women's
Movement," Caitlin Flanagan pointed out that the professional woman's
problem of housework, first identified by Betty Friedan, had been resolved
"like magic, as though the fairy godmother of women's liberation had
waved a starry wand [and] the whole problem got solved [by] the forces
of global capitalism." Such realities posed moral dilemmas for a movement that prided itself on egalitarianism. As Naomi Wolf bemoaned:

> I never thought I would become one of those women who took up
> a foreordained place in a hierarchy of class and gender. Yet here we
> were, to my horror and complicity, shaping our new family struc-
> ture along class and gender lines – daddy at work, mommy and
> caregiver from two different economic classes, sharing the baby
> work during the day.

As Flanagan dryly observes: "She had wanted a revolution; what she got
was a Venezuelan." Flanagan goes on to cite the *New York Times* columnist
Susan Chira, who claims a solidarity between privileged professional

women and the "generations of black women [who] had to work, and ... [whose] children saw their work as evidence of devotion, not neglect." "Well, you know those black women," says Flanagan sardonically, "they have all the luck." That claim of an identity of interest between those who *want* to, and those who *have* to, work is also present in Australia:

> There are a number of women living on islands in the South Pacific who adore children and would like to come to Australia to help us look after ours. They want to bounce Australian kids on their knees, peel bananas and mangoes for them and teach them to play simple musical instruments. They love to sing lullabies ... they love little kids. They were raised in a culture where family is important. They are kind, gentle and often speak some English. They can play pat-a-cake all day.
>
> There is an army of highly paid, highly qualified, very frustrated professional women in Australia who want to hire them ... Business loved the idea, saying they could put the men to work, picking fruit. Parents could put the women to work, doing household chores and taking care of the children. The islanders would get jobs that pay more, with better conditions than they can get at home. Unionists were apoplectic, saying it amounted to exploitation of brown-skinned people. Can't they ever look at the bright side?

You might think this is from a nineteenth-century plantation owner, but it is from a 21st-century columnist, Caroline Overington at the *Australian*.

In modern societies, an educated, skilled, disciplined and motivated workforce is one of the most important components of national wealth. In 1995, the World Bank estimated that 59 per cent of the wealth in developed countries is embodied in human and social capital. Although many people contribute – grandparents, teachers, fathers and child-care workers – mothers, who are usually the primary caregivers, are the most important influence in children's development of their "human capital."

Women's unpaid work – the "dark matter in the universe of labour" – makes a huge, unrecognised contribution to economic life. Duncan Ironmonger's investigations during the '90s showed that at least half of all Australian economic production came from unpaid work within households. The Australian Bureau of Statistics calculated that the value of unpaid work was between 48 and 64 per cent of GDP, while German studies give figures of up to 55 per cent. While women are not the only providers of non-market labour, they do more of it than anyone else. Roughly two-thirds of their time is spent on non-market work, and one-third on market work. For men the proportions are reversed.

As women have joined the workforce, the full "worth of a wife" has become more evident. It is more difficult for women with family responsibilities (and without wives!) to succeed in the workforce in the same numbers as men with non-working wives. Many more career women than career men are childless. All this suggests that women face trade-offs and hard choices that men don't. Yet as women's earning capacity and their investment in marketable skills have increased, so too has the perception that time out from the labour force raising children is time wasted. Here is an example of such thinking:

> As a woman does not work in certain periods, less working experience is accumulated. Moreover during periods of non-participation, the human capital stock suffers from additional depreciation due to a lack of maintenance.

Needless to say, the investment women make in caring for others does not count here as the development of "human capital stock." If a mother breastfeeds her baby, it does not add to GDP. If a mother works and gets a day-care worker to care for her baby, it does count. In fact, undervaluing women's labour and their lives is written into our very accounting systems, which measure a society's wealth by the size of GDP or goods and services bought and sold, leaving out a huge amount of what goes into our wellbeing.

Economic discussions of human capital emphasise investment in one's own skills at the expense of investing in one's children's. A mother's marginalisation in the workplace is usually shrugged off as one of life's inevitable compromises. It is mothers rather than childless women who remain unequal in the labour market. Whoever cares for the kids will suffer the care penalty.

When everything is for sale, as Nancy Folbre remarks, "women in particular begin to wonder why so much of the work they do goes unrewarded." The danger of this is that we will all become too selfish, unleashing the "war of all against all." Individualism and the new capitalism as value systems give men no real incentive to change. Instead, all the incentive is on the side of remaining competitive in the workplace and in life, by devolving care responsibilities onto others. Yet the needs of the sick, the young and the elderly remain, competing with an ever more demanding workplace which demands a player "off field" looking after the needs of every player "on field" at work. This leaves working mothers with insoluble problems in balancing care and work.

The care penalty for doing the right thing by others – the earnings forgone; the opportunities lost; the poverty in old age in the event of divorce; even the loss of esteem in the eyes of the world – is harsher than ever. It has been estimated that a well-educated American woman with a college degree who stays home to look after the kids can expect to forego up to one million dollars in potential earnings. It is not just staying home with the kids. The difficulties faced by both at-home mothers and working mothers have the same source – the devaluation of care. Working mothers also suffer a care penalty, in terms of promotions, being available for the plum jobs, and so on. In order to care for their families well, they rush around after work seeking to accomplish all the manifold tasks of running a household. The devaluation of that work, and ideal worker norms, allow employers to be unsympathetic or even punitive towards those with significant caregiving responsibilities.

Meanwhile, the rewards for behaving selfishly have also escalated. Too many women find themselves in the grip of the "nice person's dilemma." Their sacrifices of behalf of others go unrequited, make them vulnerable to exploitation, and in the event of divorce to poverty. Opportunists in an individualist paradise can take advantage of those who are generous and co-operative. In the short term, such a society can survive. In the long term, many potential caregivers will begin to recognise what is valued, where benefits are directed, and where the care penalty lies. There is a real question as to how much of modern society's dramatic decline in fertility is related to the care penalty. The problem, according to Folbre, is that we are increasingly creating a world not just with a new "economic environment" but also a "new social ecology," one where "individualistic competition for wealth offers no rewards for the work of care." We must "distribute responsibilities for care more equally and reward caring more generously ... [and] show how we might do this – in practice as well as theory."

Global warming is a looming catastrophe. The cause is not just human activity and the burning of fossil fuels. It derives from a fatal flaw in our system of accounting. We track social progress by narrow measurements of economic growth and GDP. We do not measure the cost of that growth in terms of climate change. The polluting power station counts as a contributor to GDP, but the safety of our environment is not counted.

Before too long, of course, this blinkered economistic thinking has profound economic consequences. The never-ending drought besetting much of Australia, or Hurricane Katrina, dramatically confronts us with the folly of our obsession with growth at the expense of every other aspect of human existence. Mainstream assessment bodies, including the OECD, are now recognising this point. Many of the things we routinely count as progress, such as rising income, higher consumption and economic activity, actively contribute to rising temperatures. Polluters can free-ride on all of us by not paying for cleaning up their act. Renewable energy needs to be re-priced, to reflect the vital non-market value of a cleaner environment. Even at the devoutly neo-liberal OECD, they have begun arguing for a re-evaluation:

> "Nothing exists until it is measured." This keen observation by the Danish physicist and Nobel laureate, Niels Bohr, has become something of a leitmotiv in the statistics world, but it bears some scrutiny … Statistics are information, but as Albert Einstein put it, "information is not knowledge." Climate change is a good example. Economic growth is another case in point. What does gross domestic product really tell us about economic and social progress? Not much. As the late Robert Kennedy remarked, such an indicator "does not capture the health of our children, the quality of their education, or the joy of their play – it measures everything, in short, except that which makes life worthwhile."

The new capitalism, in the short term, makes for a vibrant, economically vital and efficient society. Long term, however, that society cannot replace itself. We have taken the shadow economy of care for granted and treated those women, in and out of the workforce who provide it, carelessly. For the care economy depends not only on altruism but also on reciprocity. It has a gritty economic dimension. Children are not just a private matter, but also a crucial part of intergenerational reciprocity. It is by families having enough children that our society provides collectively, through their taxes as adult workers, for all of us in old age.

And having children is just what we are not doing. Most Western nations face a crisis of reproduction. Falling fertility – the grey dawn, as it is called – has profound implications. The central issue is the potentially shrinking pool of workers supporting dependents, whether they be children or the elderly. Soon a shrinking working-age group will support a large cohort of ageing baby-boomers.

In all Western nations, to a greater or lesser degree, fertility is in long-term decline. The causes are complex and multiple, the cure uncertain. The facts, however, are dramatic. Even in pro-family Catholic states such as Italy and Spain, the fertility rate is currently 1.2. By mid-century the size of the Italian population over sixty will double and those aged over sixty-five will outnumber children seven to one. In Australia our fertility rate is less dire, at 1.8, but still of great concern. Societies need about 2.1 children per woman per lifetime to reproduce themselves.

Falling fertility is directly related to the ways children, child-rearing and the non-market value of family work are not counted in our systems of accounting. It derives from precisely the same problem as global warming. Women going into the workforce are counted as contributing to rising GDP. Yet despite the blithe confidence of those promulgating the Get to Work program, unless conditions are very carefully thought through, societies adopting it will encounter a version of the demographic winter faced by the Eastern European countries that adopted, post-war, the "employment for all" approach. Simply providing child-care and short maternity leaves was not enough.

Sweden, Norway, Finland and France, too, have found that if you aim at high female employment, fertility will fall unless you adopt generous pro-natalist policies which include labour-market regulation with generous provision for time off for care. That means longer paid parental leaves, part-time work, and support for care of sick children, aged-care and so on. Otherwise, mothers may feel that the double burden is all too hard and restrict themselves to just one child.

This is not just a "moral" argument about the wrongs of devaluing care, important though that is. By thoughtlessly imposing a penalty on those who invest in the generations to come, we invite potentially disastrous economic effects as fertility falls. We have to find ways of attributing economic value to non-market reproductive activities – like having and rearing children – which profoundly affect the economy, in both the short and the long term.

When seen through the narrow lens of a proponent of the Get to Work program, a woman who bears and cares full time for five children is an economically irrational and unproductive citizen. She is worth "less" because she is outside the paid workforce. A childless career woman, or one who obeys Hirshman's Rules and has just one child, viewed through such a lens, is of more value to society. The other way of looking at the homemaker is that she is contributing in a different way, not just in terms of rearing children and the value of unpaid work, but simply by having children.

The childless dual-career couple, if prosperous, are likely to have a more comfortable old age, while the homemaker (especially if she divorces) is more likely to have a penurious one. Yet it is her children's taxes and their labour that enable both financial provision for social security and the care needed for the childless couple's old age. In a nutshell, we have foolishly arrived at a society where there is an economic disincentive to have and care for children, but an economic incentive to restrict fertility and instead invest in one's own skills and income. It is the irrationality of rational economics.

It is falling fertility, however, above all else, which gives women a political bargaining chip of a new and powerful kind. Policy makers, formerly deaf to mothers' needs, will have no choice but to listen.

In an essay in *The Monthly*, Kevin Rudd wrote that "the time has come for a vision for Australia not limited by the narrowest of definitions of our national self-interest." The family must not be "sacrificed at the altar of market reality ... progressive politics argues that the mandate of the state goes beyond the exclusive celebration of the self ... a properly functioning society embraces the interests of both self and other – not just the first to the absolute exclusion of the second."

He is right. What we need is a new societal deal, one that both opens the world of work to women, but respects love's labour in the shadow economy of care. Rudd's sense that we must create the social and economic foundations on which we can fulfil our responsibilities to others has common ground with what I have been arguing here. It deepens and extends our contemporary discussions of family and work. It highlights the fact that while we must create more opportunities for women to flourish, there are very different ways of achieving that aim.

The two most important versions of the new gender contract that we need to consider are the social-democratic and the neo-liberal. Both Scandinavia and the United States have high rates of women working, yet they are implementing the new gender contract and organising care in very different ways.

Despite the conservatism of the Bush administration, the rates of women participating in the workforce are among the highest in OECD nations. The United States has the largest number of elite women doing well (11 per cent of managers) and the least sex-segregated workforce. All this, however, comes at a price. There is a widespread "care crisis." There is also a moral price, ironic in terms of the universal and egalitarian aims of the early women's movement. Care and household work have been transferred to poorer women and women of colour.

Medical benefits are tied to full-time work. There is a housing affordability crisis. Business interests dominate. It took eleven years of intense political struggle to achieve a meagre three months of unpaid family and medical leave; consequently, many mothers must return to work soon after childbirth. Welfare mothers in some American states are *forced* back to work as early as three months. Child-care is provided by the market in for-profit centres, where quality is often poor. The US National Institute of Child Health and Human Development estimated that only 9 per cent of child-care was good quality. Breastfeeding is on average of shorter duration than in countries that have paid leave. Child and maternal poverty rates are among the worst in OECD nations. The plight of elderly women – many of whom have given their lives to care – is particularly dire. This is a society that puts work centre-stage, marginalises caregiving and penalises those who provide it.

The social-democratic model is far more promising. Take its treatment of parents. For Scandinavian parents of very young children under three, either parent can take up to three years' parental leave, much of it paid. They have the right to return to their previous job. They have the choice of a high quality child-care place or taking a home-care allowance. Interestingly, where it has been introduced, the home-care allowance has been extremely popular. Very few babies are in child-care. Breastfeeding rates are high. The Swedes also offer the right to work six-hour days on reduced salary until a child is eight. All these measures are regarded as *parents' and children's rights*. While no society has yet perfectly resolved the clash between the competing priorities of work and children, this policy regime achieves much more than the neo-liberal one. Maternal and child poverty is the lowest among OECD nations.

We are at an historic turning point in the relation between family and work. Here the cautionary tale of the Blair government is instructive. Early in its term of office it embraced the Get to Work neo-liberal program: early return to work for women, rapidly expanding child-care places. Yet following growing international evidence on the diversity of women's preferences, and in particular the new research showing that child-care in the first two years of life can create problems for child well-being, it changed course to one closer to the social-democratic path. Patricia Hewitt, then British trade and industry secretary, admitted late in 2003:

> If I look back over the last six years I do think that we have given the impression that we think all mothers should be out to work, preferably full-time as soon as their children are a few months old. We have got to move to a position where as a society and as a government we recognise and we value the unpaid work that people do within their families.

Britain has extended parental leave to two years, aiming at one year of paid leave, and granted the right to request part-time or flexible work to parents of children under six. More than a million parents, one-quarter of those eligible, made such requests in the first year alone.

Australia could embrace similar policies. Here are some of the things we should do:

- *Adopt active neutrality as the guiding principle of family policy.* Governments should support the plural nature of modern families, without trying to engineer choices about the balance struck between family life and work.

- *Bring in maternal equity policies based on choice.* The state should be neutral on women's different choices, offering a choice between a child-care place and an equivalent cash benefit as a home-care allowance.

- *Extend parental leave.* Australia's present one year of parental leave should be immediately expanded to two years, with an eventual aim of three years. In European countries, this is the most significant policy, which helps parents balance work and family, and aids fertility. It recognises preferences, the importance for many women of a long-term connection with the labour force, and the problems sometimes associated with child-care.

- *Establish early-childhood centres.* Transcend the current narrow emphasis on centre-based child-care. Create neighbourhood parent and child centres. The idea is to seek to surround *all* parents and *all* children with support from birth onwards. The centres would be focal points for parents to create their own community networks, as well as the contact point for referral to professional services: pre-natal visits, maternal nurses, mother's groups, babysitting co-ops, toy libraries, playgroups, as well as professional outreach services.

- *Introduce the right to request part-time work and flexible work for family reasons.* This should be available throughout the life cycle, not just during early childhood.

- *Improve the quality of child-care.* Improving child-care quality is not just a matter of subsidising corporate child-care. We should alter our regulations and attach extra funding to enforce a ratio of one care-giver per three babies in line with overseas best practice. Support for the non-profit community sector should be expanded, not least because it can offer high quality benchmarks for care undistorted by the profit motive.

- *Integrate new understandings from attachment research into child-care.* This provides the best shot in the locker to achieve high quality child-care. All caregivers will need to be trained to understand attachment principles. Because so much of a child's world is mediated through relationships, because their emotional, social and cognitive development are plaited together, it is the sensitivity and responsiveness of the child's *relationships* which matters most. There should also be a "primary care" model, whereby one person looks after the baby, a second person is assigned to each child in the event of the first being ill or absent, and the primary carer stays with the group until the children are three.

- *Reduce length of day and speed of entry into child-care.* This involves a reorganisation of many of our contemporary work and child-care practices. Many mothers have to go back to a full day of work and also commute. That means a baby — at the height of separation anxiety — spending up to ten hours per day in child-care. Only a bureaucracy could have designed a policy so insensitive to infant needs. Instead, we should support gradual entry into child-care by granting parents the right to work shorter days during the transition.

- *Keep centres small and the overall number of children low.* The "quality" of substitute care is not simply determined by structural matters such as ratios and caregiver turnover, although of course these matter. Research is showing that as well as high ratios of caregivers to babies, groups must be small.

- *Pay child-care workers more.* Caregiving is a highly skilled job; hence child-care workers need to be trained, respected and paid better than they are presently or we will never improve the endemic problem of caregiver turnover.

- *Establish universal pre-school.* Part-time educational programs for four- and five-year-olds should be voluntary, free and universal. Present provision is patchy, especially in New South Wales and in disadvantaged areas, where it is needed most. The latter also may need targeted intervention projects and home-visiting programs. Attention, however, should be paid to the quality of pre-school services provided in child-care centres.

- *Strengthen the quality accreditation standards.* We need an accreditation system with teeth, involving random, on-the-spot inspections of child-care centres and tougher penalties for violations.

While I have concentrated here on early childhood, the challenge to integrate work and family life is much broader than this. Many similar problems bedevil aged care in a market society. As the baby-boomers age, this aspect of the care deficit will deepen.

We need to go beyond band-aid solutions, such as short periods of paid maternity leave, to create a radical new social imagination around care. Instead of advocating self-sufficiency for all, we should recognise our interdependence. Devaluing parenting and care as a "lesser life" helps no one. All of us, deep down, know that in small and large acts, men and women must take responsibility for each other. Together, we must knit the fabric of care for those who depend upon us. All that takes time. All this deserves time.

And equality? We will truly have equality when women no longer have to make impossible choices. When they are everywhere in public life and when both men and women are respected for their contribution to love's never-ending labour. It is only then that being female will be felt as a presence and not an absence.

SOURCES

3   "I've never asked Therese": cited in AAP news report, "Marriage Stronger than Ever: Rudd," *Sydney Morning Herald*, 28 May 2007.

3   "an independent business woman": cited in Carla Danaher, "Rudd Offensive, Claim Mums," *Herald Sun*, 26 May 2007.

3   "British sociologist of women's work": Catherine Hakim, *Work Lifestyle Choices in the 21st Century*, Oxford University Press, New York, 2001.

4   "Rein is pretty stock standard": Natasha Cica, "Playing the Politics of Distraction," *Age*, 29 May 2007.

4   "There was a period of time where I was a stay-at-home mum": cited in AAP news report, "Therese Rein was a Stay at Home Mum," *Brisbane Times*, 26 May 2007.

4–5   "women must have the right to choose": cited in AAP news report, "Therese Rein was a Stay at Home Mum."

5   "What I do at work is my life support": cited in Scott Casey, "Rein Defends 'Life Support'," *Age*, 26 May 2007.

5   "she was the urger, she was the encourager": cited in Simon Mann and Kate Askew, "The Thing about Therese," *Age*, 24 April 2007.

6   "It seemed suddenly possible": Barbara Pocock, *The Work/Life Collision*, Federation Press, Annandale, 2003.

7   "a striking intervention in the mother wars": Linda Hirshman, "Homeward Bound," *American Prospect*, 21 November 2005.

7   "the so-called 'opt-out revolution'": Lisa Belkin, "The Opt-Out Revolution," *New York Times*, 16 October 2003.

7   "put work first, marry beneath you": Suzanne Goldenberg, "In the World of Self-Imposed Mental Enslavement," *Guardian*, 14 January 2006.

7   "The best way to treat work seriously is to find the money": Linda Hirshman, "Homeward Bound."

9   "Soon she had a blog, a book contract": Linda Hirshman, *Get to Work! A Manifesto for Women of the World*, Penguin, New York, 2006.

10   "While Hirshman complained in an injured tone": Linda Hirshman, "Unleashing the Wrath of Stay-at-Home Moms," *Washington Post*, 18 June 2006. The web article she complains about is: "Everybody Hates Linda," by Judith Stadtman Tucker, available at <www.mothersmovement.org/features/05/hirshman/homebound_1.htm>.

10   "farewells to maternalism": Ann Shola Orloff, "From Maternalism to 'Employment for All': State Policies to Promote Women's Employment across

the Affluent Democracies," *The State after Statism,* ed. Jonah Levy, Harvard University Press, Cambridge, Massachusetts; London, England, 2006.

11   "Putting sick people to work was an instance of 'social inclusion'": Shaun Carney and Michelle Grattan, "Upbeat Costello Spells Out Vision for his Australia," *Age,* 15 September 2007.

12   "get women back into the workforce as quickly as possible": Kenneth Davidson, "Child Care on the Cheap is Bad Policy," *Age,* 25 October 2007.

12   "European Commission (EC) and the International Labour Office (ILO) repeatedly endorse": Catherine Hakim, *Work Lifestyle Choices in the 21st Century,* p. 125.

12   "One headline in 2005 screamed": David Uren, "Costello: Get Mums Working," *Australian,* 1 April 2005.

12   "welfare-to-work reform has the *noble* goal": George Megalogenis, "Howard's Restless Battlers," *Australian,* 9 October 2007.

13   "The women's movement was": for a fuller explication of this argument see my book, *Motherhood: How Should We Care for Our Children?,* Allen & Unwin, Sydney, 2005.

14   "equality as sameness has got us so far but not far enough": Jane Waldfogel is a U.S. economist, cited in Ann Crittenden, *The Price of Motherhood: Why the Most Important Job in The World Is Still the Least Valued,* Henry Holt and Company, New York, 2001, p. 44.

14   "Treat me as a person": Raimond Gaita, *A Common Humanity: Thinking about Love & Truth & Justice,* Text Publishing, Melbourne, 1999, p. 72.

14–15 "as if childcare were equivalent to dishwashing": Ann Crittenden, *The Price of Motherhood,* p. 62.

17–18 "Yet in here we strike a similar paradox": Hester Eisenstein, "A Dangerous Liaison? Feminism and Corporate Globalisation," *Science and Society,* vol. 69 (3), July 2005, pp. 487–518.

18   "feminism has been abducted": Arlie Hochschild, *The Commercialisation of Intimate Life: Notes from Home and Work,* University of California, Berkeley; Los Angeles, 2003, p. 13.

18   "The 'new capitalism' is a term coined": Richard Sennett, *Respect: The Formation of Character in an Age of Inequality,* Penguin, London, 2003.

18   "'Affluenza,' the luxury fever of conspicuous consumption": see Clive Hamilton's forceful critiques of "affluenza," in his *Growth Fetish,* Allen & Unwin, Crows Nest, 2003.

19   "Social policies based on the male-breadwinner model of the family": from "A Caring World," quoted in Rianne Mahon, "The OECD and the Reconciliation

Agenda: Competing Blueprints," Childcare Resource & Research Unit, University of Toronto, Occasional Paper 20, July 2005. (Originally presented at a conference held 7–8 January 2005, St Anne's College, University of Oxford. Available at <www.childcarecanada.org/pubs/op20/op20.pdf>.)

19   "In the new capitalism, work has become sacred": Helen Trinca & Catherine Fox, Better Than Sex: How a Whole Generation Became Hooked on Work, Random House, Sydney, 2004.

19   "Work has taken on an enchanted quality": Arlie Hochschild, The Time Bind: When Work Becomes Home and Home Becomes Work, Metropolitan Books, New York, 1997, p. 44.

19–20   "it was all about the 'sanctification of work'": Ross Gittins, "Work: Less an Ethic, More an Order," Sydney Morning Herald, 8 June 2005.

20   "we have to work": Don Edgar quoted in Daniel Donahoo, Idolising Children, University of New South Wales Press, Sydney, 2007.

20   "In their 2003 book": Elizabeth Warren and Amelia Warren Tyagi, The Two-Income Trap: Why Middle-Class Mothers and Fathers are Going Broke, Basic Books, New York, 2003.

21   "we have seen a housing affordability crisis": Mike Steketee, "Wealth is Up but so is Your Mortgage," Australian, 28 June 2007.

21   "individualism and choice are supposed to stop abruptly at the boundaries": Anthony Giddens, The Third Way: The Renewal of Social Democracy, Polity Press, Cambridge, 1998, p. 15.

21–22   "In their report": John Ashcroft, Bill Hurditch, Michael Diamond and Paul Shepanski, An Unexpected Tragedy, Relationships Australia, 2007, available at <www.relationshipsforum.org.au/report/index.html#unexpected_tragedy>.

24–25   "Betty Friedan once told Simone de Beauvoir": conversation between Betty Friedan and de Beauvoir cited in Christina Hoff Sommers, Who Stole Feminism?, Simon & Schuster, New York, 1994, p. 257.

25–26   "stay-at-home dad": David McKnight, Beyond Right and Left: New Politics and the Culture Wars, Allen & Unwin, Sydney, 2005, pp. 184–5.

29   "the kind Betty Friedan advocated in 'A New Life Plan'": Betty Friedan, The Feminine Mystique, Penguin, Middlesex, 1963, p. 302.

29   "A Good Weekend feature in 2002": Jane Cadzow, "Kids? What Kids?" Good Weekend, Age, 17 August 2002.

30   "Male-styled careers": Arlie Hochschild, The Commercialisation of Intimate Life, p. 238.

31   "outpouring of women's grief": Virginia Hausegger, "The sins of our feminist mothers," Age, 22 July 2002.

31   "It suits us to let mothers": Judy Wacjman, *Managing Like a Man: Women and Men in Corporate Management*, Penn State University Press, Pennsylvania, 1998.

32   "Weren't you Ann Crittenden?": Ann Crittenden, *The Price of Motherhood*, p. 12.

32–33 "There's just a disappearance of mum": Pru Goward in interview with Michael Cathcart, *Australia Forum: "What's a Nice Girl Like You Doing in a Job Like This?"*, 2 November 2003, available at <www.abc.net.au/rn/bigideas/stories/2003/976820.htm>.

35   "My observations about the differences": for fuller discussion of these matters, see my book, *Motherhood*, chapter 5.

35   "hardhat empirical studies": Catherine Hakim, *Work Lifestyle Choices in the 21st Century*. See also Catherine Hakim, *Key Issues in Women's Work: Female Diversity and the Polarisation of Women's Employment*, *Glasshouse Press*, London, 2004, which is an expanded second edition of a book first published in 1996. For a controversial early article, see Catherine Hakim, "Five Feminist Myths about Women's Employment," *British Journal of Sociology*, vol. 46, pp. 429–55.

35   "We all believed it": Catherine Hakim cited in Bettina Arndt, "Myths and Misconceptions," *Sydney Morning Herald*, 7 February 2003.

36   "Despite being commissioned": Catherine Hakim "Competing Family Models: Competing Social Policies," paper delivered to annual Australian Institute of Family Studies conference 2003, available at <www.aifs.gov.au/institute/pubs/fm2003/fm64.html>. See also Catherine Hakim, "Taking Women Seriously," *People and Place*, vol. 9 (4), 2001.

36   "Lastly, there was a shift": Anthony Giddens in his Preface to Catherine Hakim, *Work Lifestyle Choices in the 21st Century*.

37   "according to the principles of modern society": for his argument see John Stuart Mill, *The Subjection of Women*, 1869, chapter 1.

37   "How women are to live": Hakim's argument is given in most detail in Catherine Hakim, *Work Lifestyle Choices in the 21st Century*.

37–38 "scathing about relying on data": see also my critique of Peter McDonald and others for using such figures in Anne Manne, "Women's Preferences, Fertility and Family Policy: the Case for Diversity," *People and Place*, vol. 9 (4), 2001, pp. 6–25.

38   "family-centred reality of women's work patterns": Angela Shanahan, "Families Worth the Work," *Inquirer*, *Australian*, 20 October 2007.

38   "Ann Crittenden shows that": Ann Crittenden, *The Price of Motherhood*, end note, chapter 2, note 10, p. 282.

38   "Social class changes the standpoint": Deborah Keys, "Complex Lives: Young Motherhood, Homelessness and Partner Relationships," *Journal of the Association*

for Research on Mothering, "Young Mothers", vol. 9 (1), 2007.

39   "Similar judgments about motherhood": Kathryn Edin and Maria Kefalas, *Promises I Can Keep: Why Poor Women put Motherhood before Marriage*, University of California Press, Berkeley; Los Angeles, 2005.

39   "Well-educated, affluent women don't necessarily agree": Daphne de Marneffe, *Maternal Desire: On Children, Love and Inner Life*, Little Brown and Company, New York, 2004, p. 25.

40   "If you offered the average parent": Tanya Plibersek, "Child Care is Not the Answer When We Need Family Time," *Sydney Morning Herald*, 29 December 2003.

40   "On this question": for information on home care allowances see Catherine Hakim, *Work Lifestyle Choices in the 21st Century*, chapter 8, esp. p. 233. Also S. Ilmakunnus, "Public Policy and Child Care Choice," in Inga Persson and Christina Jonung eds, *The Economics of the Family and Family Policies*, Routledge, London, 1997.

40   "I think the government's very conscious": Pru Goward in interview with Michael Cathcart, Australia Forum: *"What's a Nice Girl Like You Doing in a Job Like This?"*

40   "In every country where information is collected": see Mariah Evans and Jonathon Kelley, "Employment for Mother's of Pre-School Children: Evidence from Australia and 23 Other Nations," *People and Place*, vol. 9 (3), 2001. Also Mariah Evans and Jonathan Kelley, "Changes in Public Attitudes to Maternal Employment: Australia 1984 to 2001," *People and Place*, vol. 10 (1), 2002, pp. 42–57.

41   "this was seen as a major financial sacrifice": Mariah Evans and Jonathan Kelley, "Changes in Public Attitudes to Maternal Employment".

41   "a mere 7 per cent": Australian Bureau of Statistics, 4402.0 – Childcare, June 2005, 95 per cent of children who use preschool attend less than 20 hours a week: ABS, 4102.0 – *Australian Social Trends*, 2004.

42   "It was the same proportion": Australian Bureau of Statistics, 4402.0 – *Childcare*.

43   "One of the best books summarising for the layperson": Sue Gerhardt, *Why Love Matters*, Brunner & Routledge, Hove and New York, 2004. See also my outline of child development for the layperson in *Motherhood*, part two, "Taking Children Seriously," pp. 111–239.

43   "The most important magic ingredient": Dr Jack Shonkoff cited in Jo Chandler, "Spare the early education dollar … spoil the child," *Age*, 3 March 2006.

44   "There is no such thing as a baby": Donald Winnicott in Clare Winnicott, Ray

Shepherd & Madeleine Davis (eds), *Psycho-analytic explorations*, Harvard University Press, Cambridge, 1989, p. 54.

44   "Their expectations of others are benign": for attachment and its importance, see Robert Karen, *Becoming Attached: First Relationships and How They Shape Our Capacity to Love*, Oxford University Press, Oxford and New York, 1994; Allan Schore, *Affect Regulation and the Repair of The Self*, W.W. Norton & Company, New York and London, 2003; Allan Schore, *Affect Dysregulation & Disorders of The Self*, W.W. Norton & Co, New York and London, 2003, esp. chapter 9.

44   "A human infant is": Lauren Porter, "The Ties that Bond: Brain Development, Bonding and the Creation of Relationships," Paper delivered to the Australian Breast Feeding Association, Warrnambool, Australia, 14 February 2008.

45   "It's no good trying to tell and admonish a child": Robert Karen, *Becoming Attached*, pp. 194–195.

45   "When infant researcher": Daniel Stern, *The Interpersonal World of the Infant*, Basic Books, New York, 1985, pp. 151–152.

46   "an experiment done by Edward Tronick": see Daniel Stern, *The Interpersonal World of the Infant*, p. 102.

46   "As the psychologist Ron Lally says": Ron Lally, U.S. early childcare specialist, in interview with Jennifer Byrne, *7.30 Report*, 6 November 1998.

46   "the capacity for emotional regulation": see Allan Schore on emotional regulation, *Affect Regulation and the Origin of The Self: the Neurobiology of Emotional Development*, Lawrence Erlbaum Associates, Hillsdale, New Jersey, 1994; *Affect Dysregulation & Disorders of the Self*; and Sue Gerhardt, *Why Love Matters*.

48   "A feeling state can become a trait": Bruce Perry, noted child-trauma specialist, is cited in Robin Karr-Morse and Meredith S. Wiley, *Tracing the Roots of Violence*, Atlantic Monthly Press, New York, 1997, p. 199.

48   "the 'full-commodification' solution": Joan Williams, *Unbending Gender: Why Work and Family Conflict and What to do about it*, Oxford University Press, Oxford and New York, 2000, chapter 2, esp. pp. 40–63.

48   "The reason lies less with its merits": Bruce Fuller, *Standardising Childhood: the Political and Cultural Struggle over Early Childhood*, Stanford University Press, Stanford, California, 2007. Fuller's book explores Weber's great insight about the rationalisation and bureaucratisation of everyday life by looking at the attempt to centrally organise, regulate, standardise and institutionalise early childhood by the universal 0–5 pre-kindergarten movement in the U.S.

49   "It's a very contentious area": Sue Gerhardt interviewed by Kenan Malik on "Catch Them Young," Radio 4's *Analysis*, 26 August 2004.

50   "It's rubbish to say we have quality child-care in Australia": Pam Cahir quoted

in Gerald Tooth, "Child-Care Profits," *Background Briefing*, ABC Radio National, 3 October 2004, available at <www.abc.net.au/rn/talks/bbing/stories/s1214400. htm>.

51   "Long term this has the potential": Sarah E. Watamura, Bonny Donzella, Jan Alwin, Megan R. Gunnar, Susan Parker and Sarah Lane, "Morning-to-Afternoon Increases in Cortisol Concentrations for Infants and Toddlers at Child-Care: Age Differences and Behavioural Correlates," *Child Development*, vol. 74 (4), July–August, 2003, pp. 1006–20; Andrea C. Dettling, Megan R. Gunnar and Bonny Donzella, "Cortisol Levels of Young Children in Full-Day Child-Care Centres: Relations with Age and Temperament," in *Psychoneuroendocrinology*, vol. 24, 1999, pp. 519–36; Andrea Dettling, Susan Parker, Sarah Lane, Anne Sebanc and Megan R. Gunnar, "Quality of Care and Temperament Determine Changes in Cortisol," *Psychoneuroendocrinology* vol. 25, 2000, pp. 819–836. See also this meta-analysis of articles published on cortisol and daycare, Harriet J. Vermeer and Marinus H. van Ijzendoorn, "Children's Elevated Cortisol Levels At Daycare: A Review and Meta-analysis," *Early Childhood Research Quarterly* vol. 21, 2006, pp. 390–401.

51   "studied children in": Margaret Sims, Andrew Guilfoyle & Trevor Parry, "Children's Well-Being in Child-Care," paper presented at the Australian Institute of Family Studies Conference, Melbourne, 9 February 2005.

51   "Even in centres considered 'satisfactory'": Margaret Sims, Andrew Guilfoyle and Trevor Parry, "Children's Well-Being in Child-Care"; and Margaret Sims, Andrew Guilfoyle and Trevor Parry, "Children's Cortisol Levels and Quality of Child-Care Provision," *Child: Care, Health and Development*, vol. 32 (4), 2006, pp. 453–466.

51   "cortisol levels of separated babies": Lucy Ward, "Hidden Stress of the Nursery Age," *Guardian*, 19 September 2005. Also, Lieselotte Ahnert, Michael E. Lamb "Shared Care: Establishing a Balance Between Home and Child-Care Settings," *Child Development*, vol. 74 (4), 2003, pp. 1044–49.

52   "Since the late 1980s": See my account of this literature and debates in *Motherhood*, chapters 9 and 10.

52   "This evidence does *not* apply": in Australia the influential advocacy group for children, NIFTEY (National Investment For The Early Years), acknowledges the risks for infants especially when the hours are longer in NIFTEY, *What About the Kids?*, 2006. Available at <www.niftey.cyh.com/Documents/PDF/Summary_FINAL-Web_Artwork.pdf>.

52   "More time in care predicts less harmonious": NICHD Early Child-Care Research Network, "Child-Care and Mother–Child Interaction in First Three

Years of Life," *Developmental Psychology*, vol. 35, 1999, pp. 1399–1413.

52   "When the study children were assessed": NICHD Early Child-Care Research Network, "Does Amount of Time Spent in Child-Care Predict Socioemotional Adjustment During the Transition to Kindergarten?", *Child Development*, vol. 74, 2003, pp. 976–1005.

53   "Children who had experienced": NICHD Early Child-Care Research Network, "Early Child-Care and Children's Development in the Primary Grades: Follow Up Results from the NICHD Study of Early Child-Care," *American Educational Research Journal*, vol. 43, 2005, pp. 537–570. Also, NICHD Early Child-Care Research Network, "Age of Entry to Kindergarten and Children's Academic Achievement and Socioemotional Development," *Early Education & Development*, vol. 18, 2007, pp. 337–368.

In 2005, a Dutch study examined the NICHD data again comparing familial care, including fathers and grandparents as well as mothers, with child-care centres. The Netherlands team found that separating out fathers and grandparents from commercial child-care predicted even more strongly the link between increased "problem behaviours and aggression in pre-school, especially in boys."

53   "more extensive non–parental care": Kay Margetts, "Children Bring More to School than Their Backpacks: Starting School Down Under," *Journal of European Early Childhood Education Research Monograph: Transitions* 1, 2003, pp. 5–14. See also "The Longitudinal Study of Australian Children" Linda Harrison, "The Child-Care Question: Is Social–Emotional Development at Age 2–3 years Affected by Children's Experience of Non-Parental Care?", paper presented at the inaugural Growing Up in Australia: Longitudinal Study of Australian Children (LSAC) Research Conference, Melbourne, 3–4 December 2007.

53   "Higher quality care reduced": E.C. Melhuish, K. Sylva, P. Sammons, I. Siraj-Blatchford and B. Taggart, "The Effective Provision of Pre-school Education Project, Technical Paper 7: Social/Behavioural and Cognitive Development at 3–4 years in Relation to Family Background," Institute of Education/DfES, London, 2001. Also, P. Sammons, R. Smees, B. Taggart, K. Sylva, E.C. Melhuish, I. Siraj-Blatchford and K. Elliot, "The Effective Provision of Pre-School Education Project, Technical Paper 8b: Measuring the Impact on Children's Social Behavioural Development over the Pre-School Years," Institute of Education/DfES, London, 2003.

54   "after reviewing other recent studies": NICHD Early Child-Care Research Network, "Does Amount of Time Spent in Child-Care Predict Socioemotional Adjustment During the Transition to Kindergarten?", pp. 976–1005.

54   "Two more large-scale studies": the Canadian study found child and parental wellbeing declined after the introduction of a universal $5 a day, child-care program in Quebec. Michael Baker (University of Toronto), Jonathan Gruber (MIT) and Kevin Milligan (University of British Columbia), "Universal Child-Care, Maternal Labor Supply and Family Well-Being," National Bureau of Economic Research (NBER) Paper, available at <http://www.chass.utoronto.ca/cepa/childcare.oct2005.final2.pdf>.

54   "also reported negative emotional and behavioural problems": Susanna Loeb, Margaret Bridges, Daphna Bassok, Bruce Fuller and Russ Rumberger, "How Much is Too Much? The Effects of Duration and Intensity of Child-Care Experiences," *Economics of Education Review* (forthcoming).

54–55 "Quality child-care in the 'early years'": See this and other similar statements in Jennifer Buckingham, "Child-Care – Who Benefits?" Centre for Independent Studies, Issue Analysis 89, 24 October 2007.

55   "for every $1 invested in child-care": Don Edgar, "The Phony Debate Forgets About Kids," *Age*, 16 June 2006.

55   "It was not ordinary day-care": Lawrence Schweinhart, Jeanne Montie, Zongping Xiang, W. Steven Barnett, Clive Belfield and Milagros Nores, *Lifetime Effects: The High/Scope Perry Preschool Study Through Age 40*, High Scope Press, Ypsilanti Michigan, 2005

56   "The cost-benefit figures": Helen Penn, Veronica Burton, Eva Lloyd, Miranda Mugford, Sylvia Potter and Sahirun Sayeed, "What is Known about the Long-Term Economic Impact of Centre-Based Early Childhood Interventions?" EPPI-Centre, Social Science Research Unit at the Institute of Education, University of London, London, March 2006.

56   "Science doesn't support universality": see James Heckman's comments available at <http://blogs.wsj.com/economics/2007/08/08/the-economics-of-pre-school/>.

57   "not necessarily disinterested": Alison Clarke Stewart's comments, " I wanted to find that child-care was good …" made to Tom Zoellner, "Daycare: Study Putting Your Kids in Daycare," *Men's Health*, 1 September 1999, quoted in Brian Robertson, *The Daycare Deception: What the Child-Care Establishment Isn't Telling Us*, Encounter Books, San Francisco, 2003, p. 58.

57   "a fascinating paper": Rianne Mahon, "The OECD and the Reconciliation Agenda: Competing Blueprints," Occasional Paper 20, Child-Care Resource & Research Unit, University of Toronto, Canada, 2005.

58   "addressing a World Bank symposium": Charles Coffey, Executive Vice President, Government Affairs & Business Development, RBC Financial Group,

"An Investment in ECD: The Economic Argument, A Better Start is Likely to Lead to a Better Finish," addressing World Bank Forum, *Symposium on Early Child Development (ECD): A Priority for Sustained Economic Growth and Equity*, Washington DC, 28 September 2005.

60   "The Swedish case is very revealing": E.C. Melhuish, quoted in Madeleine Bunting, "Nursery Tales: Are Nurseries Bad for Our Kids?", *Guardian*, 8 July 2004, available at <http://education.guardian.co.uk/schools/story/0,,1256424,00.html> and <http://www.guardian.co.uk/politics/2004/jul/08/research.earlyyearseducation>.

62   "the author of this parable": Nancy Folbre, *The Invisible Heart: Economics and Family*, The New Press, New York, 2001, p. 22–23.

62   "a central issue of our time": Arlie Hochschild, *The Commercialisation of Intimate Life*, p. 3.

63   "Not cutting it – that's pretty much the gist": Madeleine Bunting, "Our Culture of Contempt for Parenthood," *Guardian*, 7 March 2006.

63   "We don't choose, we have to": Leo Shanahan, "$500 Extra, but Carers just Want Some Dignity," *Age*, 24 October 2007.

63   "Today patriarchal coercion is unacceptable": Nancy Folbre, *The Invisible Heart*, pp. 20–21.

64   "philosopher and mother of a profoundly disabled child": see Eva Feder Kittay's important book, *Love's Labor: Essays on Women, Equality, and Dependency*, Routledge, New York and London, 1999. Martha Nussbaum has acknowledged the challenges posed to her capabilities approach by Kittay's dependency theory – see the symposium on Eva Kittay's *Love's Labor* in the feminist journal *Hypatia*, vol. 17, 2002.

64   "These feminists": Dorothy Roberts, "Care's Critics: Addressing Feminist Arguments against Public Support for Carework," Fourth Annual Carework Network Conference, 13 August 2004. Also, "The Subject of Care: Feminist Perspectives on Dependency," Eva Feder Kittay and Ellen K. Feder (eds.), Rowman & Littlefield Publishers, Lanham, 2002.

65   "Yet applied to the relational world": Jennifer Roback Morse, *Love and Economics: Why The Laissez-faire Family Doesn't Work*, Spence Publishing Company, Dallas, Texas, 2001.

66   "Even if the actual decision-makers": Nancy Folbre, *The Invisible Heart*, p. 149.

66   "the fairy godmother of women's liberation": Caitlin Flanagan, "How Serfdom Saved the Women's Movement," *Atlantic Monthly*, February 2004.

67   "They love to sing lullabies": Caroline Overington, "We Ought to be Sharing Our Bounty," see her blog on the *Australian* website, 13 December 2006,

available at: <http://blogs.theaustralian.news.com.au/coverington/index.php/theaustralian/comments/job/>.

67   "the most important influence in children's development": Ann Crittenden, *The Price of Motherhood*. "The dark matter in the universe of labour" is Crittenden's phrase in *The Price of Motherhood*, p. 47. She also gives an extremely clear and persuasive account of the "disappearing" of mothers' labour in chapters 3 and 4.

68   "the human capital stock suffers from additional depreciation": Ann Crittenden, *The Price of Motherhood*, p. 4.

69   "expect to forego up to one million dollars": Ann Crittenden, *The Price of Motherhood*, p. 5.

70   "new social ecology": Nancy Folbre, *The Invisible Heart*, p. 18.

71   "but it bears some scrutiny": Donald J. Johnston, Secretary-General of the OECD, March 2005, "Statistics, Knowledge and Progress," *OECD Observer*, no. 246–247, December 2004–January 2005.

72   "In Australia our fertility rate is less dire": for longer discussion see Anne Manne, "Women's Preferences, Fertility and Family Policy".

74   "a properly functioning society embraces": Kevin Rudd, "Faith in Politics," *The Monthly*, October 2007.

76   "all mothers should be out to work": Patricia Hewett quoted in Rachel Sylvester, "Working Mothers Demand Choice to Stay at Home," *Daily Telegraph*, 15 October 2003.

79   "We need to go beyond band-aid solutions": Human Rights and Equal Opportunity Commission, Discussion Paper, *Striking the Balance: Women, Men, Work and Family*, Sydney, 2005. See also, Human Rights and Equal Opportunity Commission, "Valuing Parenthood, Options for Paid Maternity Leave: Interim Paper," Sydney, 2002.

Correspondence

Bill Bowtell

"*We* can win the election, but *he* cannot," was Peter Costello's blunt assessment of the Coalition's prospects were John Howard to lead it into the 2007 election.

A year ago, not many observers of Australian politics agreed with Costello. Most professional commentators were sure that John Howard would coast to an easy victory on the back of a buoyant economy. They dismissed Costello as a self-interested Cassandra (perhaps forgetting that Cassandra was proven correct). One of the few who shared Costello's view was the long-time historian and scholar of the Liberal Party, Judith Brett.

She believed that the times no longer suited John Howard and was convinced that he would not prevail against Kevin Rudd.

Backing her conviction, Brett staked her claim on the first post-election *Quarterly Essay* to explain the reasons for John Howard's defeat. In it, she argued persuasively that John Howard was simply too old, too dogmatic and too out of touch with the shifting centre of Australian public opinion to counteract Kevin Rudd's drive, dynamism and fresh-faced appeal.

Yet her compelling *Quarterly Essay* also points the way to an explanation for the Howard government's decline and fall that is more complex and more significant than the argument that ageing leaders are generally unable to come to terms with their own obsolescence.

The most significant question posed by the 2007 debacle is precisely why did the Liberal Party throw it all away. Why, when all the economic winds were set fair, and the political shoals to be negotiated were not especially hazardous, did the crew of the Liberal ship of state allow its captain to steer indefatigably to the extreme right? Even when the cliffs loomed above them, and disaster was imminent, why did they not toss Howard overboard and set a new course?

Was Peter Costello right in asserting that the election was winnable for the government but only without John Howard? Or was it the case, as Judith Brett believes, that the Liberal Party no longer had the means or the will to act independently of its leader?

Costello was understandably keen to succeed to the prime ministership rather than become leader of the opposition. Throughout 2007, he stridently made the case for John Howard's early departure to his party colleagues and the press gallery and, through them, to the public. He asserted that a simple change of leader was all that was required for the Coalition government to prevail at the 2007 election. Costello might have been acting from self-interest, but he also had the weight of evidence on his side. From the day of Kevin Rudd's elevation to the Labor leadership, the direction of the polls was undeniably wretched news for the Coalition government. Rudd and the Labor Party maintained handsome leads over Howard and the government. As the months wore on and the polls did not shift, there could be no reasonable doubt that the Howard administration would be resoundingly defeated at the elections. But Costello's case for change failed. Prepared to wound, but unwilling to strike, Costello destabilised the Howard government and undermined John Howard's legitimacy but was unable to persuade his colleagues to install him in the leadership. At the time, this failure was attributed solely to Costello's personal unpopularity with the Australian public. Yet Costello and his backers also seriously misjudged the wider political environment. They assumed that the Australian people believed that the Coalition government's policies, priorities and entire political project were worth supporting at the 2007 election and that the only thing that stood in the way of the government's re-election was John Howard. This was not so. In 2007, the Australian people were intent on repudiating not just the Prime Minister but also the government itself. As deputy architect of the government's political project, Costello represented continuity, not change. A change in leadership without a change in the policy settings of the government was tantamount to no change at all. This insoluble conundrum petrified and paralysed the Coalition government throughout 2007.

In early 2007, Brett was far more sanguine and realistic in her assessment of the situation than Costello. As a long-time observer of the Liberal Party, she was perforce a student of John Howard's character and personality. John Howard had been at the heart of Liberal Party politics for four decades, including eleven years as the party's leader and prime minister. Far more than has ever been possible for any leader of the Labor Party, John Howard had come to dominate, control and shape his party. A year ago, she divined that the Liberal Party would be incapable of shifting Howard if he did not want to go. She foresaw that the Mexican stand-off between Howard and Costello would continue indefinitely and could not be broken save by Howard's resignation.

Unlike Brett, Costello clearly failed to grasp just how completely Howard had shaped the Liberal Party in his own image and to suit his own purposes.

For better, and, as it turned out, for worse, the Liberal Party saw its fate as inseparable from that of its leader. Costello gave them fair warning, and a plausible alternative, but his colleagues opted for martyrdom nevertheless. They knew what he did not. That he was serving in the Howard government, not the Howard–Costello government or even the Howard Liberal government. The powers that be within the Liberal Party had somehow persuaded themselves that without John Howard, the government he led had no meaning, purpose or hope of a separate, continuing existence.

In her essay, Brett outlines how effectively John Howard deconstructed the old Liberal Party he inherited in 1996. Over the Howard years, the Liberal Party degenerated from a political party into a movement supporting a quasi-presidential leader. The parliamentary Liberal Party became even more of a cheer chamber and less of a check on executive excess than in previous Liberal administrations. As she vividly recounts, by 2007 the Liberal Party had become little more than a sort of low-rent Australian Peronist movement, subservient and responsive only to the whims, enthusiasms and prejudices of its leader. The zenith, or the nadir, of this metamorphosis was the high farce of the attempted leadership putsch at the time of the Sydney APEC meeting. How revealing that, unlike all other prime ministerial or party leadership spills, this one was played out not in and around the parliament in Canberra but in a city literally in a state of South American-style siege. All that was missing were the tanks. The parliamentary members of the Liberal Party were neither involved nor informed as the Cabinet convened in several secret sessions to plot the overthrow of its leader. As we now know, their pathetic entreaties to Howard to depart were finally turned down contemptuously not just by him, but, in a moment worthy of Evita, by Mrs Howard as well. How simply astounding that grown men and women, the heirs and successors to the vibrantly diverse party bequeathed to them by Menzies, Holt, Gorton and Fraser, should have so meekly acquiesced in their own political destruction.

John Howard's staring down of his putative political assassins was, of course, a testament to the strength of his own self-belief as well as to the utter weakness and lack of resolve of his opponents.

But this clash of personalities and egos masked something perhaps rather more troubling and disturbing in the evolution of one of the two great and enduring parties of Australian democracy.

Had the Liberal Party sustained its once deep and wide roots in Australian society, over the course of the Howard years two broad factions would have emerged in the parliamentary Liberal Party. These currents of opinion would have reflected both the extreme right neo-conservatism pursued by Howard and his allies since 1996, and a more traditional liberalism more drawn from the broad centre of Australian society.

After a decade of neo-conservative ascendancy, it was clear that by 2007 the tide had swung back to the centre and left and away from the right. On a succession of issues – the Hicks and Haneef cases, the support of the invasion and occupation of Iraq, the contemptuous dismissal of the reality of global warming, the decline of the public health and education systems and the introduction of WorkChoices – John Howard had moved very far away from the centre of the Australian political spectrum.

In the nature of things, over time a functional and healthy political party would have brought forth a political and personal alternative to Howard's neo-conservatism.

Yet this did not happen.

Howard cannot remotely be blamed for hanging on to the leadership for as long as he could. But something is deeply wrong with a party that could not axe a leader whose time was up and whose policies were generally no longer supported by the Australian public. That no such political alternative emerged demonstrates how completely Howard and his allies had purged their ideological foes.

The Liberal implosion of 2007 therefore had its more distant origins in the destruction in the early 1990s of the old Liberal Party at the hands of Howard, Costello, Kroger and their party and business supporters.

Howard and Costello were both highly conservative neo-liberal warriors who shared a deep hostility to old-fashioned liberalism. In 2007, Peter Costello could not toss John Howard because the public knew that there was no serious political, as distinct from personal, difference between them. And the largely powerless residual structures of the old Liberal Party could not toss either of them because Howard and Costello had purged the parliamentary Liberal Party of liberals, leaving only those who supported the neo-conservative line relentlessly pursued by the Howard government since 1996.

It was policies not personalities that brought down the Howard government. And, more to the point, it was Howard's embrace of American neo-conservatism, and the public's rejection of it, that culminated in the political massacre of November 2007.

In the early 1990s, Howard and his allies transplanted this foul exotic bloom from the American hothouses of neo-conservatism, run by and for the most extreme elements of the United States Republican Party, to the ideological desert that was the Australian Liberal Party after a decade in opposition.

Over most of his pre-prime ministerial career, John Howard was an incipient neo-conservative and had been so even before the term was invented. But as the neo-con revolution gathered strength and pace in the United States, so did John Howard's commitment strengthen to the revolutionary causes of unrestricted free markets, low income taxation, high indirect taxation, general privatisation of public assets and the restoration of social orthodoxy that the neo-conservatives believed had been overthrown in the libidinous 1960s.

When he fought the 1996 election, Howard was, of course, too canny and elliptical to proclaim publicly his fealty to the neo-conservative cause. In 1996, he was elected on the ultimate "me too" platform. He gave no hint that he intended to impose a neo-conservative agenda on an unsuspecting Australian electorate, reassured by his apparent devotion to "relaxed and comfortable" business as usual. In office, however, he moved swiftly and decisively to the far right, and never again came back to the centre ground of Australian politics. From the time of his election onwards, there can be no doubting that his purpose was to bring about the political, social and economic transformation of Australia along neo-conservative lines.

But, predictably enough, American neo-conservatism never found a congenial home under Australian skies or took root in Australian society.

Australia is not America.

Try as Howard did, Australian society was not easily going to be transformed into a free-market, deregulated, low-taxing, devil-take-the hindmost facsimile of Texas.

As early as the 1998 election, it was obvious that the Australian people rejected Howard's neo-conservative vision for Australia. At that election, a majority of the Australian people voted him out of office, but he clung on to power thanks to the Australian electoral system's inability to translate a majority of votes into a majority of seats.

Howard recklessly interpreted his 1998 near-death experience as a reason to press forward to his ultimate goal. As Brett notes, Howard grew more determined to govern from the extreme right, using the tried and tested techniques of fostering division, discord and fear. Like his patron, George W. Bush, John Howard was a master of wedge politics. Instructed and inspired by his Republican mentors, Howard and his acolytes ceaselessly laboured to inflame public opinion against convenient scapegoats – Muslims, Aboriginals, homosexuals and single mothers – while pretending to speak for "mainstream" values.

But his public support wavered, then deeply eroded, as he implemented the core elements of the neo-con policy handbook – massive income-tax cuts, the introduction of the GST, cripplingly high fees for tertiary education, ill-thought-out privatisation of public assets and redistribution of spending from the poor to the rich. After his nominal election loss in 1998, Howard prevailed in two more elections but both times in exceptional circumstances. In 2001, the September 11 attacks on the United States produced a surge in support for neo-conservative militarism that, in Australia, evaporated as soon as Howard supported the disastrous American invasion of Iraq. In 2004, Labor scored an own goal by presenting an alternative leader whose incapacities became obvious only when it was too late to replace him.

These two fluked victories were trumpeted by Howard's media and business supporters as ringing endorsements of the neo-conservative policies of the Howard government. They were nothing of the sort.

Yet none of this weighed on Howard, or slowed the pace at which he pursued his increasingly radical policy agenda. The apotheosis of Australian neo-conservatism came with the profound ideological assault on the working conditions of low- and middle-income families known as WorkChoices. WorkChoices irreparably broke the already frayed link of consent between the Howard government and those it governed. WorkChoices sealed the fate of the Howard Liberal government. It was the last straw in the pile of hay bales that Howard had loaded on to the backs of the Australian people since 1996. From that point on, the government's, and not just John Howard's, demise was as certain as anything in politics can be.

While the fall of the Howard government occurred in 2007, the long strange death of Liberalism therefore began with the purging of centrists and liberals from its ranks in the 1990s. The mid-1990s triumph of economically and socially extreme elements in many Liberal branches played a major role in the consequent collapse of the Liberals at every level of municipal, territorial and state government and, eventually, at the federal level as well.

The ruination of the Liberals took place in full public view over more than a decade. No national existential crisis caused the demise of traditional Liberalism or the collapse of the Howard government. Indeed, it perished during a time of unprecedented prosperity and confidence. The portents, warning signs and klaxons never ceased flashing and sounding, yet the Howard neo-conservative caravan pressed cheerfully on from disaster to disaster and then into oblivion. It passed into history unmourned, unloved and unlamented.

Australian Liberalism collapsed because it turned its back on its own history and spurned its deep political roots in Australian culture and society. With eyes wide open, the Liberal Party rejected its traditional pragmatic centrism to embrace the most extreme variants of a romantic, utopian ideology imported by Howard and his followers as a total design for living from a far distant, rather alien, society.

In 1996, Howard hocked the future of the Coalition government to an extreme political philosophy that was then already discredited but that by 2007 was all but defunct in America itself. He gambled that Australians could be persuaded away from being a northern European-style social democracy to becoming something more like the southern United States.

In November 2007, he lost the bet and with it his government.

The clearest lesson of the 2007 debacle is that there is no future in Australian politics for a socially and economically hard-line neo-conservative party or at least not one that aspires to form national government.

Whether, how, and indeed why the remnants of Australian Liberalism might rise from the disaster of the Howard years remains an open question and one which I hope that Judith Brett might soon address.

Bill Bowtell

Correspondence

Norman Abjorensen

In between Judith Brett's insightful *Relaxed and Comfortable* and her incisive *Exit Right* we have the eerily fascinating Errington and van Onselen biography of John Howard – but still we see through a glass darkly.

I call the biography "eerily fascinating" because it is essentially about a man who does not exist; there is only a politician, albeit a driven, determined and ruthless one, who connives and plots and intrigues instead of living. We peer in vain into that space behind the politician and instead of a man we find an endless repetition of the looking-glass kings in *Macbeth* – but they are all John Howard, politician.

There is something of Dame Edna superstar here – the suburban man writ large; but to my mind there are three extraordinary things about Mr Ordinary (if that is not a contradiction).

The most extraordinary thing about Howard is not that he managed to lose the 2007 election entirely off his own bat, or even that he won four elections on the trot. No, the extraordinary thing is that he even became prime minister in the first place.

The second most extraordinary thing is that he represented himself with some success as a "man of the people," insisting that it was he alone who had a direct line to the heartland of middle Australia, that he was "in touch" with the average Australian in a way that no one else was. It was, and remains, a chilling conceit; quite the nearest thing we have had in Australia to that primitive Germanic concept of the General Will.

The third thing is that Howard managed for a decade to entice half of the Australian voting public (except in 1998) to enter into a private fantasy world that he had built over decades of resentment and then projected onto the Australian electorate as an authentic construction of national life.

Let us take these points one at a time. How did Howard become prime minister? As in real life, Howard PM had two parents: the father was Paul Keating, the progenitor of the worthy Big Picture, but a leader quite lacking in either the political or the communication skills to take the electorate with him; instead of transmitting enthusiasm, Keating sowed resentment in all those who felt they were not part of his scenario. This resentment created the political space for Howard. (It was not the only wayward offspring generated by Keating; Pauline Hanson and One Nation share a common paternity). The mother of Howard PM was a shamelessly promiscuous Liberal Party, seducing and abandoning lovers who could not deliver the coveted riches of power. Peacock had failed twice, Howard had been cut out by a wayward National Party premier, Hewson had been promised two terms but had been unceremoniously ejected after one, and an absurd dalliance with callow youth saw the surreal leadership of Alexander Downer. Howard, ambitious as ever, was still standing and allowed himself to be drafted. He was what Bill Hayden memorably called the "drover's dog" – someone who could have been anyone handed an election there for the taking, as was Bob Hawke after Hayden resigned on the eve of the 1983 election.

How "of the people" was Howard? He had, by any standards, led a sheltered life, socially and intellectually. From working in the family service station to his entry into the legal world, Howard never experienced the brutal authoritarian vicissitudes of the workplace that are everyday life for most Australians. He had, by all accounts, never been harassed, bullied, humiliated or sacked by a boss or manager, never resented the arbitrary power that bosses use against workers. Did he ever take a "sickie"? That he was so out of touch with workaday Australians was confirmed by his quip when explaining the rationale behind his abolition of unfair-dismissal laws – that every workplace had a "pain in the neck," and why should they be protected? How strange that this passed with so little comment: many Australians would have thought the "pain in the neck" was the boss.

The world according to Howard was, as Brett points out so rightly, constructed on the "primal opposition" between Liberal and Labor; it was a Manichean view of all of social life, not just politics, that so pervasively inflected Howard's thought and deed. It was whatever gang he could muster against Labor (and he managed, it has to be conceded, some fair numbers in 1996, 2001 and 2004).

Labor, of course, was weak for much of the Howard ascendancy, just as Labor had been weak as well as divided for much of the age of Robert Menzies from 1949 to 1966, and this was a potent factor in Howard's success, just as it was for Menzies'. Labor's weakness was, in part, self-inflicted, partly through indifferent leadership but more so from a misplaced loyalty that prevented the party from repudiating Keating; this cost Labor dearly. Howard's deft use of the political "wedge" in prising away a slice of working-class support from Labor worked as he systematically derided the "new class," the "elites" and the dreaded "political correctness" as being linked to the ALP brand.

The incursion Howard made into Labor's heartland was derived from his own political life experience as much as it was from political necessity: Labor's cultural networks, of which the unions were a key part, had to be demonised, neutralised and eliminated. He succeeded in the first, for a time in the second, but the third remains unachieved.

Consider Howard's world. He was born in 1939 in Sydney, just as the ramshackle and squabbling coalition that had come into office in New South Wales after Lang's dismissal in 1932 and the subsequent implosion in the ALP was itself unravelling. The new social coalition put together by the still under-rated Bill McKell in 1941 saw Labor sweep into office and hold on to power for a record twenty-four years.

What this quarter of a century of ALP rule did in an admittedly Labor state was to extend and consolidate not just electoral power but political power in the widest sense – in the unions, in local government, in the churches, in the universities and even in some business sectors. It was patronage at its most powerful, and it was entrenched and hard to dislodge, as even eleven years of Liberal government from 1965 to 1976 left little mark on it.

It was James Jupp who many years ago identified the "out-group" mentality of the Liberal Party in New South Wales and its right-wing "ratbag" proclivity, and it sprang from the same well as Howard: everywhere the Liberals looked in New South Wales, they saw Labor; it was permanent siege mentality. It was not so much a political fight, as the more self-confident Deakinite Victorians tended to see it, but a cultural one as well as an existential one.

It was this, along with the narrow, small-business shopkeeper mentality that shaped Howard's world, and he retailed this to the rest of Australia. A telling passage in the Errington and van Onselen biography reveals Howard's resentment at his father's plight in being involved in a planning dispute over the siting of petrol pumps. To Howard, this was merely petty officialdom, inspired of course by the Labor ethos that had no respect for small business. It never crossed his mind that there might have been a greater public good involved, and this thinking coloured his whole political career, especially his prime ministership. Howard's curiously close and uncritical relationship with capitalism – quite unlike that of the sceptic Menzies – cries out for further exploration.

Howard, clearly, has left the Liberal Party in a parlous state (and Menzies would not be pleased). Not only has he left it leaderless at the national level,

Brendan Nelson notwithstanding, he has played a key role in the party's political demise in the states. First, he has bled the states of resources and whatever talent there was; second, he has insisted on unquestioning acolytes running the state divisions; and finally his neo-liberal policy prescriptions have proved to be electoral poison at the state level where government equates with service delivery. Howard has always insisted he is a creature of the Liberal Party, but under his watch in his home state it has been taken over by unelectable extremists. The 2007 state election in New South Wales was certainly the nadir of the party, as it failed to land a glove on an inept, incompetent, untalented and possibly corrupt ALP administration.

Even Howard, the consummate political animal, failed to sniff the political wind; the man whose political instincts and sheer determination had carried him to the top succumbed to hubris, misreading signs all around him. Concern over climate change had taken hold in the electorate and he realised this – unconvincingly – far too late. Similarly, he failed to notice the groundswell of concern over David Hicks – again until too late.

He also believed he had seen Beazley off; the public had simply stopped listening to him. Did it never occur to Howard that he was about to suffer the same fate? Indeed, it may well be that by the time Rudd was elected leader at the end of 2006, Howard was already becoming inaudible; Rudd's ascension simply turned the volume switch off.

In pondering Howard's legacy, Brett concedes that while the Liberal Party is damaged and the nation is singularly unprepared for readjustment in the face of climate change, Howard at least "has left Australia with a booming economy, and most Australians are more prosperous than they have ever been." But is this really the case? The *Australian Financial Review* reported on 24 January that 60 per cent of our GDP comes from consumer spending, and any slackening would impact immediately on economic growth. Think about that for a moment: in an age of absurdly easy credit (à la sub-prime) we are afloat on a sea of four-wheel drives, holiday houses, boats and plasma televisions, all financed with borrowed funds at historically (but temporarily) low interest rates. Much of the prosperity is illusory, and the illusion can be easily shattered, which poses the question about the nature of a legacy that preaches public fiscal rectitude (except during election campaigns) while not just encouraging but demanding rampant profligacy by consumers wallowing in a morass of debt, owning little but owing much. Any way you look at it the whole process is unsustainable.

Finally, Brett and others are too inclined toward generosity in their musing over Howard's reluctance to hand over to Costello. The humble, loyal and selfless (but also, as Brett notes, defiant) servant of the party – "there only so long as the party wants me" – was played over and over in the media, said with a straight face with the earnest hangdog Honest John matter-of-fact expression, and taken at face value; whereas it was a taunt, as boastful as it was cynical.

The surreal side of this was Howard as the increasingly erratic King Lear; the *Realpolitik* of it was Howard as the Liberal Party's bolshevik Lenin: he had the numbers, menshevik Costello did not.

Howard never let up being a politician, not for a moment; this was his undoing. His own limited life experience precluded him from ever seeing Work-Choices as many Australians did; it was not his Australia. Rather than try to understand this, he simply dismissed it from his consciousness as a mere figment of a Labor–union campaign.

Howard never really knew us at all – only the parts he wanted to know.

Norman Abjorensen

Rebecca Huntley

Reading Judith Brett's *Exit Right* in the last week of 2007 was a fitting end to a memorable year in Australian politics. I was reminded while reading Brett of Peter Hartcher's thesis in the first QE of the year, *Bipolar Nation*. In that essay, Hartcher proposed that Howard would win the 2007 election on the twin pillars of economic management and national security. I was in the audience at a Gleebooks event in April when Hartcher was interviewed by Maxine McKew. McKew had agreed to the engagement shortly before announcing her candidature for the seat of Bennelong; on the night of the event she fronted up to a large audience eager to hear what the Prime Minister's challenger had to say about Labor's chances. Instead of a leisurely talk between fellow journalists, the event turned into Hartcher interviewing McKew about why his thesis was flawed. Her argument? Yes, economic times were good and governments are rarely ditched by electorates under such circumstances. But these were, as McKew asserted, "extraordinary times," particularly in terms of the environment and the workplace. Looking back over the year, it seems that while Hartcher's prediction was wrong, his thesis was generally sound. Economic management *was* critical to the result in the 2007 election, but not in ways that particularly advantaged the Coalition. And the issues of terrorism specifically and national security generally did not feature in voters' minds in the way they had in previous elections, preoccupied as they were with industrial fairness, rising food and petrol prices, global warming and water.

Brett's meticulous chronicle of the Coalition's *annus horribilis* makes these points and more. It's difficult to quibble with such a thorough analysis. Except that, like all political junkies, Brett is interested in the jousting of question time, the nuances in the leaders' debate and the posturing at APEC in a way few voters are. What becomes clear when you conduct any kind of research into social attitudes and trends is that the mini-dramas and minutiae of partisan politics comes across as meaningless static to most Australians. They try, and often succeed, in blocking it out. At best it creates a mere backdrop to decision-making about whom to vote for, a process that often happens months before an election is called, fought and won.

Indeed, the conditions for a change of government were all present in early 2007. In the focus-group research I and others conducted then for *The Ipsos Mackay Report*, we encountered fatigue with a government that seemed to be out of ideas and even at odds with the public mood on key issues. One of those issues was obviously the environment. Brett states that "it is not yet clear why public opinion had shifted so decisively by mid-2006" on this issue. From our research, what was clear is that voters were starting to make a crucial link between the global phenomenon of climate change and domestic concerns such as water shortages, drought and extreme weather. They perceived that environmental problems were already affecting their daily lives in the form of water restrictions and rising food prices. Among many voters there was a perception, and a subsequent anger, that because governments hadn't acknowledged the problem and planned for the future, Australian consumers would be faced with higher prices for staples, water and energy. Suddenly it felt as if climate change would hit the back-pocket, sooner and harder than expected. In the face of all this, the conventional opposition between "the environment" on the one hand and "the economy" on the other didn't seem to hold. The distinction wasn't simple. Al Gore made this point graphically in his documentary – money or the world? It's a false choice, and many Australians were beginning to sense this.

It was intriguing to watch the sustained interest throughout 2007 in how first-time and younger voters were going to swing. Intriguing because young voters are usually ignored or dismissed as ill-informed or apathetic. They haven't got the numbers or the clout of the Boomers or the self-funded retirees, and so rarely merit attention from political parties focused on percentages. In previous elections, Howard had claimed the Gen Y cohort as some of his greatest supporters; certainly they had grown up with only dim memories of a Labor prime minister. And yet 2007 saw a small but significant shift among the late teens and early twenties from disengagement to engagement. Rudd's lead over Howard among these voters cannot be attributed (as Brett partially does) to *The Chaser* boys' pranks or party propaganda transmitted via Facebook or YouTube. Rather, it was the convergence of particular policy issues (specifically the environment, workplace security and faster broadband) and the compelling argument for generational change that I believe really won this group over. Of course Rudd's work on FM radio and his eleventh-hour appearance on *Rove* didn't hurt. But I believe that you underestimate the nous of young voters if you think that this is all it takes to win them over. Returning home late on election night, I listened as my neighbour, a 23-year-old girl with a penchant for fluffy dogs and havaianas, tearfully expressed to me how excited she was that Australia had, in her words, "made the right choice for my generation."

Another issue touched on by Brett that merits further consideration is the public's complex attitude to unions – and the ALP's complex relationship with the union movement. Brett argues that "the government's rhetoric on union power was out of line with public perceptions" and that Australians are more supportive of unions than they are suspicious of their power. Brett also asserts, as other commentators have, that in relation to unions the Coalition pursued two contradictory lines of argument during the campaign: one, that unions are irrelevant in today's society, and two, that unions wield too much power. I see no such contradiction. Union membership remains in decline. Even the introduction of WorkChoices didn't see a significant spike in their numbers. From our research it seems as if many Australians expected the government, not the unions, to protect them from unscrupulous employers; thus in the wake of WorkChoices they punished the government rather than joined union ranks. In terms of benefit to the community, many Australians may well view unions as no more or no less useful to society than any NGO that fights for social justice or any organisation that seeks to benefit its members. Their clout is diminished. And yet, as a consequence of their affiliation fees and conference delegate numbers, they have greater power within the ALP than they do outside it. Not, as the Coalition would have you believe, to dictate policy. But largely to ensure that the most powerful (usually male) union secretaries in the land make a fairly cruisy transition into parliament. This is a problem. For every talented Greg Combet there is a much less talented comrade promoted, often in advance of other candidates who could make more valuable contributions. The Coalition ads targeting the large number of former union officials on the front bench (and in the caucus) were not disturbing because these members were once union officials. They were disturbing because they revealed that Labor's parliamentary contingent is unrepresentative of the broader community. It would have been just as worrying had it been shown that former dentists dominated the shadow ministry. It is this skewed and narrow profile of Labor's parliamentary wing that so concerned thinking Laborites during the drab and desolate years of Beazley et al.

In his 2006 Quarterly Essay *What's Left?*, Clive Hamilton argued that the federal ALP had run out of ideas and that Australia needed a new party concerned about the environment, willing and able to espouse a progressive politics not based solely on economic growth and deprivation. He said the federal ALP was moribund. Two years later it's enjoying its most successful political period since its foundation (if we judge success by being and staying in government in every state, territory and now at the federal level). The irony in all of this is that the ALP is still much the same beast as it was during its long period in federal opposition. Few of the structural and cultural problems that its thinkers and members agonised over during the wilderness years have been addressed. As the Prime Minister and his team knuckle down to the hard work of government, I imagine all these concerns will be set aside until, inevitably, Labor's fortunes change.

Rebecca Huntley

Tony Kevin

There is an emerging consensus that John Howard lost the 2007 election primarily due to voter fears over WorkChoices, worry over interest-rate rises (and broken promises), a sense that he was getting too old for the job, and growing alienation, especially in younger voters, from his aggressively combative style of politics; the latter two factors thrown into sharper relief by Labor's choice a year before of a much younger, gentler and more affable leader. This consensus is filled out and shaped by Judith Brett's impressive essay.

I think there is something important missing, or at best undervalued, in this analysis: what I call the moral outrage factor. From about 2000 onwards, issues of breaches of public morality began to concern increasing numbers of people: slowly at first, but with an ever-increasing certainty that this was a seriously morally flawed government. Thus, by 2000, human-rights abuses in detention centres had become a public issue. In 2001 came *Tampa*, children overboard and SIEV X. In 2003, the invasion of Iraq, and the Rau and Solon cases of Australian citizens being mistreated as presumed illegal immigrants. Then came the cynical government cover-up of the AWB scandal. From 2004 onwards, the prolonged agony of David Hicks was a public issue. More and more people worried about the moral effects on the nation of a progressive demonisation of Muslims in an expanding national-security culture, and saw the Cronulla riots as confirmation of their fears. Finally in 2007 came the Haneef case. I see all these events as progressively generating in sections of public opinion a moral unease, which eventually swelled into a final firm rejection of Howard's claims to be a good leader of Australia.

Australian mainstream politics and the media pack who follow it are still uncomfortable with language that imports moral issues into the discussion of politics. Because of our history of divisive sectarianism, secularism is seen as a virtue in politics, and discussion of moral issues can be wrongly seen as an underhand effort to re-introduce the Christian religion into politics. Through most of the Howard years, on both sides of politics as well as in the media, morality tended to be dismissed, or paid perfunctory lip service in politicians' Christmas and Easter messages of varying sincerity.

The members of the media, culturally schooled to eschew moral value judgments in their work, are particularly uncomfortable with expressions of moral language in politics. So a series of uneasily humorous ways were found of putting moral critics of Howard safely in elitist or special-interest boxes: chardonnay critics, the latte set, doctors' wives, bleeding hearts, the mob, Howard-haters, etc.

Anyone who has been involved in protest activity on any of the above-mentioned list of issues will know what a travesty of truth this is. Such dissent engaged people at all levels of society from rich to poor, and of diverse political and social outlooks. One of the best indicators of the growing moral outrage against Howard, impressionistically, was the number and tone of letters to the editor published in the major dailies. Most editors of letters pages try to convey a fair balance of letters coming in, in those they select for publication. I noted between 2000 and 2007 a gradual but definite increase in the proportion of letters critical of Howard on moral grounds, often fiercely so, and a gradual drying-up of letters defending him. I hope someone one day will do a proper statistical analysis of this.

In such a finely balanced election as 2007 was, it can be said, I think accurately, that if moral issues swayed the votes of just 5 per cent of voters – that is, 1 in 20 – that would have been enough to dislodge Howard. But how to establish whether that 1 in 20 would not have voted against Howard in any case for some of the other reasons noted at the start of this letter? The published results of questionnaires about reasons for voting do not give us the answer, because that question was generally never asked.

Yet before the election both Rudd and Howard recognised the growing weight of moral issues in numbers of voters' minds. Rudd set out a careful exposition of his moral views in an essay "Faith in Politics," published in The Monthly, in a way that would have satisfied many such voters. Howard tried hard to wrap his Aboriginal child-protection intervention in a language of morality. Both leaders took pains to present themselves well at an online national Christian forum shortly before the election.

Judith Brett's essay briefly refers to some moral issues, but they are somehow missing from her overall conclusions. In a longish list of things Howard did that appalled "left-liberals," she includes "the way he … evaded responsibility for the children-overboard affair and for the scandals about the AWB, by the harshness and hypocrisy of his asylum-seeker policies." She refers to "defecting liberal Liberals with moral qualms." She notes Rudd's "Faith in Politics" essay as a good statement of his own moral claims as a politician, but she does not assess it as an implied moral critique of Howard – which it clearly also was, to those who read between the lines.

Where Brett most clearly diverges from my view that moral issues mattered in the 2007 election is in this key passage:

> Consider, too ... the excessiveness of the Howard-haters. The latter's loathing cannot be satisfactorily explained by any actual harm that his policies have done to the people who hate him, but is rather the expression of their profound alienation from the mood Howard has brought to the nation and the way he goes about the business of governing.

Here the limitations of an assumption that voter choices are mostly driven by self-interest, and perhaps also by judgments about political image or style in a particular election year, are most clear. "Howard-haters" as Brett calls them here, were actually people who felt personally distressed and shamed by the great harm they saw Howard's policies inflicting on defenceless people *other than themselves*. Whether they were proceeding from Christian or secular-humanist ethical positions, Howard's systematic cruelty brought sentiments of altruism and human solidarity into play – I think, in enough numbers of voters to make a difference in 2007.

In a well-balanced review of Brett's essay in the February 2008 issue of the *Australian Book Review*, Patrick Allington makes an important point:

> Brett's big-picture approach and her steady tone transforms the debate over the Howard government's perceived successes and failures, demanding that the nation – as well as the man – take ownership of the last eleven years.

He suggests that Brett's essay may only be her preliminary assessment, and that further work will follow "that will help us to grasp the good and the bad reasons why the electorate for so long rewarded and celebrated our own Strong Leader."

I hope that in further work, Brett will try to evaluate professionally the importance of the moral issue – how the "moral outrage" factor may have over time changed the way the electorate thought about Howard – briefly discussed here. It is important for the health of our future politics for us all to have a better understanding of when and how the nation decided that "whatever it takes" is not enough of a moral guideline for Australian governance.

Tony Kevin

Judith Brett

"When you change the government, you change the country," said Keating in 1996, warning us what to expect if John Howard were elected. Howard's version of the warning last year was more modest: "There is no such thing as a change of government when everything continues the same as it was before the change." He hoped people would fear that without him as prime minister their economic prosperity was at risk. When he won government from Labor, particularly after 1998, he certainly tried hard to change the country. And many of those who voted for Labor last year no doubt hope it will change again.

What is at stake in these claims is the nature of the relationship between the government and society, the government and the nation: in particular, the government's power to effect deep social and cultural change. Politicians, not surprisingly, believe this power to be great. Political journalists generally do too. During the eleven years in which Howard was Australia's prime minister, he spoke on behalf of the nation. Countless journalists in countless articles wrote about how Howard had changed Australia; and countless people around countless dinner tables and water coolers complained that they felt strangers in their own land and speculated about moving to New Zealand. And now he's gone.

When Rudd, on the first day of the new parliament, apologised to the Stolen Generation, their families and their communities, we again heard in the federal parliament stories of unbearable grief and terrible wrongdoing, just as we had in April and May 1997 when the Human Rights and Equal Opportunity Commission had first presented its report Bringing them home. Again settler Australians were being asked to listen, to reach out and to take some responsibility for the suffering inflicted on Indigenous Australians by the forced removal of their children. It seemed as if a huge blackboard duster was rubbing out Howard and all he had stood for: the years of mean-minded, hairsplitting word games, the dog-whistling, the poverty of spirit and moral imagination. It seemed as if the small boy with his finger in the dyke of historic denial had finally gone, and the sympathy of settler for Indigenous Australians was free to find its course; it seemed as if history had simply washed him away.

But of course it hadn't, and there was opposition leader Brendan Nelson reminding us how many Australians still see settler–Indigenous relations as Howard did. What had changed was not the country, but the government. And the prime minister.

Tony Kevin and Rebecca Huntley both focus on how to explain the election result that changed the government. Kevin argues that I underestimate the extent to which moral outrage played a part in defeating Howard and over time "changed the way *the electorate* thought about Howard." Huntley argues that from early 2007 the Ipsos Mackay researchers encountered "a fatigue with a government that seemed to be … at odds with *the public mood* on key issues." Bill Bowtell writes that "In 2007, *the Australian people* were intent on repudiating not just the Australian people but the government itself." The problem I have with all these claims is the italicised collective nouns; because only some of the electorate, some of the Australian people and some of the public changed their vote. The final swing against the government was in fact quite modest – only 5.44 per cent. The two-party-preferred vote was 47.3 to 52.7, an exact reversal of the 2004 result when Labor lost with 47.3 to the government's 52.7.

There are two things to say about this result. The first is that the Coalition did a great deal better in the final poll than in the horror opinion polls during the year, which at times showed a ten-point difference and more between the two sides. Newspolls in April and May had two-party-preferred votes of 41 to 59. To my mind the closeness of the result vindicates Howard's decision to stay on and lead the party into the election and the defeat he believed was coming. I believe that with Costello as leader, the final election result would have been far worse for the Coalition. As Bill Bowtell points out, there was little policy difference between Howard and Costello; and as the opinion polls repeatedly found, Costello had very low approval ratings as preferred prime minister. Howard would have known that he would be blamed for the defeat, and that many would argue that he should have gone. Had he gone, and the defeat been worse, he would have been blamed for that too, the rat leaving a sinking ship. Perhaps it might have worked had he handed over to Costello in 2006, though only if this had forestalled the Labor Party replacing Beazley with Rudd. Once Rudd became leader, I don't think there was much the Liberals could do except wait for Rudd to fall over, which he didn't. And I agree with Bowtell that this was as much about policies as personalities: neo-liberalism had reached its limits as the economy hit the capacity constraints of the resources boom; and Howard's transplanted neo-conservative cultural agenda had few roots. Howard did pretty well for a government without a clear policy direction and the party should be grateful to him.

The second thing to say about the 2007 election result is that it again displays the stability of the carve-up of the electorate between the two sides of Australia's party system. Only twice since the Second World War, in 1966 and 1975, has the difference between the two-party-preferred votes been greater than 10 per cent. In 1996, an election now regularly described as "a landslide" in which Australians repudiated Keating's cultural agenda, it was 46.4 to 53.6. That is, almost half the country still voted for Labor and Keating. It is the fact that at most elections more than 45 per cent of the electorate votes for the other side that makes me so uneasy with the collective nouns used in so much writing about Australian politics. Occasionally, as in 1998, when the ALP actually won 51 per cent of the two-party-preferred vote, the majority votes for the loser.

At any given historical moment the country/nation/polity includes individuals and groups with a range of ideas, feelings, beliefs and ways of being in the world. This range is finite but it is also fluid, malleable and full of contradictions and disagreements. What a party gets when it wins government is the chance, for a time, to give that range a temporary shape, to highlight some of the possibilities of the contemporary moment and to ignore others. Elected by a little over half the valid votes, after a divisive and often bitter fight, the winning side, and the prime minister in particular, gets the right to speak for the country/nation/people as a whole. This is the interplay between division and unity which is at the heart of liberal-democratic government and which I have written about before. We expect the prime minister to claim that he speaks on behalf of the country/nation/people. That is his prerogative. But we do not have to believe that in so doing he is expressing some sort of collective will.

What I disagree with in so much political commentary is the collapsing of the polity into the society, such that people read the actions and statements of politicians as straightforward evidence for the beliefs of the people. The country gets the government it deserves, they say. People who profoundly opposed Howard on the moral issues Kevin discusses blamed a country that had become hardened and morally callous. But, as we saw when Rudd said sorry, those people were still part of the country, reconciliation was still believed in and hoped for by many Australians, even as others will still hold back. As the Rudd government proceeds, we will see other political possibilities restored: like the republic, and perhaps a more independent foreign policy.

The relationship between social and political change is more complex than much political writing has the time or patience to recognise. And they move at very different speeds. Social change is mostly slow and incremental. Political change can be swift and dramatic. One day Howard is prime minister, living in Kirribilli House, the media hanging on his every word; a week later he is packing up his house and office and Rudd and his new ministers have the glow of office. What I think happens is that, in hindsight, some changes of government come to represent more general social and historical changes, and elections become useful markers for collective memory. So the 1949 election, which the Coalition won 51 to 49, or the 1972, which Labor won 52.7 to 47.3, (the same margin as in 1996 and 2007), have come to be seen as moments when the old gave way to the new. This is not because of the way people voted, which was not very different from the way they had voted in the previous election, but because of what the government did and the general direction of social change.

I agree with Rebecca Huntley that most voters are uninterested in the jousting of question time and the nuances of leaders' debates, and that the mini-dramas of partisan politics are barely even a backdrop to their voting decisions. The changes in social attitudes displayed in some changed votes are caused by experiences beyond and outside the world of politics. Even so, I think the political itself warrants close attention if we are to understand how governments succeed and fail. In Exit Right, what I wanted to do was to look at John Howard's political leadership under the pressure of the election defeat I believed was coming, not because in itself I thought this would explain the election result, but because I thought it would help us to understand how Howard had governed, and what would come after his defeat, particularly for the Liberal Party. I feel completely vindicated in my analysis by the troubles that have engulfed the federal party since it lost government. The glue of power melted far faster than I had anticipated. It is hard now to believe that Nelson and other senior members were so recently ministers of the Crown, as they dither between rising to Rudd's invitation to bipartisan consensus to tackle the emergency of Indigenous disadvantage and maintaining their right to disagree and oppose.

I also thought that as the limitations of Howard's leadership become more apparent, this would set in train political problems for him in maintaining the capacity and cohesion of his government and the confidence of the media. As it turned out, I was right about the first but not the second. For reasons I don't fully understand, many in the media maintained confidence in his capacity to win till almost the very end.

The prime minister and his ministers have many audiences for their words and actions besides the generalised electorate, specialised audiences in the media and among business and policy elites, who do focus on the nuances of speeches and the mini-dramas of partisan politics. The judgments of these audiences about the government's competence are important for the government's capacity to get things done. When a leader starts to unravel, so does the capacity of his government and his party.

I found Norman Abjorensen's contribution extremely interesting. His discussion of the NSW Liberal Party's sense of cultural siege and "outgroup" mentality gave a historical context to the energy Howard put into the cultural wars, energy that might otherwise seem to have mainly psychological sources. State differences in political culture are not well understood by any of us, nor the interaction between these state cultures and our federal governments. The aggressive divisiveness which Howard shared with Keating and which I wrote about in *Exit Right* may be a consequence of their shared NSW origins. And the relief so many of us feel now that Howard has gone may simply be that we are no longer governed from Sydney Town.

Judith Brett

Correspondence

Philip Moore

Ian Lowe's essay is strong on assertions but weak on factual evidence. He tells us that nuclear power is too expensive (p.3 and many other places), the economic case for nuclear power is very dubious and is usually based on a careful selection of past evidence or heroic assumptions about future costs (p.3), the economics don't stack up (p.19), there is no economic case for it (p.19), it is at least double and perhaps three times the price of coal and gas (p.35), it costs much more than some renewables (p.36), and economists can't see any way of making the costs look credible (p.66). There is more, but you get the point. He correctly says that comparisons of economics are difficult because the outcome depends critically on the underlying assumptions. Although this does not deter him from making dogmatic statements, it apparently excuses him from any meaningful attempt at a cost comparison.

For calculating the cost of wind power, I have used cost and performance figures from the report *Renewable Energy Used for Electricity Generation in Australia*, published by the Parliament House Parliamentary Library. For calculating nuclear costs, I have used manufacturer's information on the Westinghouse AP-1000 reactor. Capital costs are A$1.82 billion per gigawatt of installed capacity for wind and A$1.33 billion per gigawatt for nuclear. Capacity factors are respectively 20.3 per cent and 90 per cent. Design lifetimes are respectively twenty years and sixty years. Capital costs work out at 5.12 cents per kilowatt hour for wind and 0.28 cents per kilowatt hour for nuclear. On these figures, the capital cost for wind energy per unit of electricity produced is eighteen times greater than for nuclear. It would take some very heroic fudging to negate this stark difference.

Lowe says (p.3) that "when we analysed the demand for concrete, steel and other materials that would be produced [to build 36 reactors] we found that it would itself have created a crisis." All published estimates of materials and energy costs per unit of electricity produced show that these are much higher for wind and solar than for nuclear. Renewable-energy proponents invariably make comparisons on the basis of installed capacity rather than electricity produced (size matters, but is less important than output) and ignore the energy and materials costs of their favoured technologies. They also ignore the financial, materials and energy costs of stand-by generating capacity which increases as the proportion of renewable power increases. They behave similarly when calculating carbon dioxide emissions. The effects of land clearing and other construction for wind, solar and crop biofuels are ignored or greatly understated. They pretend that, when wind or solar power cuts in, they displace the worst polluters (black and brown coal) whereas they preferentially displace higher-cost, easy-to-turn-on-and-off, less-polluting, gas and hydro power. If this is insufficient to balance the grid, some coal-fired plant is put into spinning reserve, steam is vented to air and little or no carbon dioxide is avoided.

On page 4, Lowe says "The level of nuclear power then steadily declined ... By the end of the twentieth century, nuclear power looked like a dying industry." This is not true. Plants under construction were completed and others were improved, uprated in capacity and granted extended lifetimes up to sixty years. The Switkowski report (p.52) shows that the number of power reactors increased from 365 to 443 and total nuclear capacity increased from 253 to 368 gigawatts between 1985 and 2005. This was a period in which generating companies initially had excess capacity and later found that organised opposition made the construction of any large-scale generating plant too financially risky. On page 20, Lowe quotes annual rates of increase for the different forms of electricity generation and claims that "the figures tell the story." But they are deceptive: it is easy to get a high percentage increase off a low base. Worldwide, wind and solar produce 0.5 per cent of electricity whereas nuclear produces 16 per cent (23 per cent in OECD countries). I think rather that these are the figures which tell the story.

On page 21, he says that solar hot water on half the houses (actually, he says households) in Queensland would save as much electricity "as a nuclear power station would provide, and do it years before any reactor would be up and running." Do the calculation: half of 1.4 million roofs saving possibly 80 per cent of 4kWh per day saves 2.24 million kWh per day, which is about one-tenth of the daily output of a 1000MW nuclear reactor. I'll bet he was hoping nobody would bother to check! Also, how long to manufacture and install 700,000 hot-water systems?

On page 25, Lowe criticises the World Energy Council for preferring nuclear over wind and solar because neither of them could be deployed quickly enough.

He says, "This borders on the dishonest, given the likely time scale for building nuclear power stations is a decade or more, while wind turbines can be built in less than a year and a solar hot-water system could be on your roof next week." First, "a decade or more" is a figure that only a dedicated opponent would choose; four to six years is more typical. Second — and this is a whopper — Lowe equates one nuclear power station, one wind turbine and one solar hot-water system. A single 1000MW reactor produces about 8.3 million megawatt hours of electricity per year. A 3MW wind turbine (the biggest in production) produces 8.7 thousand megawatt hours per year (assuming a generous 33 per cent capacity factor at the best wind sites) and a solar hot-water system produces no electricity but could save 1.2 megawatt hours per year. If you multiply up the number of turbines and hot-water systems to compare equal outputs and their effect on carbon dioxide emissions, you will get a fairer comparison. Further down the page he says, "The fact that quite intelligent people embrace nonsense of this kind reveals ..." It is an observation that could well be turned back on its originator.

On page 27, Lowe mentions some of the criticisms made against renewables which, although he claims otherwise, have never been satisfactorily answered. He calls them "urban myths" and "no substitute for a rational energy policy," then, without explanation, states that all the Earth's people can live comfortably with a mix of renewable energies. He suggests that the 1960s are a good time to emulate. I wonder what he proposes to give up. He cites Sweden, Norway and Iceland as examples where a third to three-quarters of energy (I think he means electrical energy) is provided by renewables, but fails to mention that this energy is from hydro in Sweden and Norway and from geothermal steam in Iceland. While these are much more predictable and less intermittent than wind and solar, the scope for hydro is limited on the driest settled continent on Earth and geothermal hot rock in this country is undeveloped and likely to be remote from large electricity consumers.

On pages 31–33, he gives a long dissertation on cost discounting and attempts to show that this unduly improves current analyses of nuclear decommissioning and waste-management costs. He makes two mistakes. He accidentally shows that present value considerations favour strategies with short-term horizons more than those with a longer term investment like nuclear. Secondly, he forgets that decommissioning and waste-treatment costs for nuclear are generally included in the electricity price. They are not deferred for forty, sixty or one hundred years and handed on to our descendants. These charges, amounting to 0.1 to 0.2 cents per kilowatt hour, have accumulated large funds because of the large amounts of electricity generated. This method is not nearly so attractive for renewables, which produce much less electricity and are often already heavily subsidised by feed-in laws (5.5–9.1 cents/kWh for electricity from wind, 54.0–57.4 cents/kWh for solar for twenty years after commissioning in Germany (1 cent = 1.6 Aust cents)).

On the matter of subsidies, Lowe (p.77) raises the common complaint that renewables are starved for financial support compared to competing technologies such as coal and nuclear. Lowe comments in an Australian context that renewable technologies have "improved dramatically [since 1992], despite meagre funding compared with the resources poured into the nuclear option." This resonates with many people but is untrue, both in Australia and the world generally.

An investigation by the OECD's International Energy Agency (IEA) found that expenditure in nuclear fission research and development in IEA countries has fallen steadily since 1980 and that expenditure in renewables research and development is now more than double that for nuclear in all IEA countries except France and Japan.

In recent years, funding in Australia by the federal government for renewables totals over $2.7 billion. It includes:

- Mandatory Renewable Energy Target (MRET): over $2 billion
- additional research and development under MRET: $134 million
- Solar Cities Program: $75 million
- Low Emission Technology Fund: $500 million
- Advanced Energy Storage Fund: $20 million
- Wind Energy Forecasting Program: $14 million
- development assistance (Asia-Pacific Partnership on Clean Development and Climate): $18 million

In addition, the recently announced 15 per cent clean-energy target by 2020, which many commentators say will mainly benefit wind energy, will create a $16-billion boost for the industry. By contrast, funding since 1992 for the development of nuclear power in Australia is zero.

Before closing, I invite the reader to look again on the third-last page at one of the few (only?) attempts in the essay to explain how renewable energies will replace dirty old coal and keep us in 1960s comfort. Did you notice (as I did and Lowe did) that Diesendorf is proposing to replace a 1000MW coal-fired plant with 801MW of gas and renewables? This would require those two to be 25 per cent more efficient than the coal plant (in other words, to have a 25 per cent higher capacity factor). But renewables in Australia constitute about 10 per cent of installed capacity yet only produce 3.7 per cent of the electricity. This means that their capacity factor is only about 37 per cent of that of the major non-renewables (black and brown coal and gas). Lowe attempts to restore reality by mentioning that 2700MW of wind turbines produce the same amount of electricity as 1000MW of coal-fired capacity (which again indicates a capacity factor for wind of about 37 per cent of that for coal). So Diesendorf's 375MW of wind power is equivalent to 139MW of coal-fired power and he is therefore claiming that 426MW of gas and biofuels can replace 861MW of coal-fired generation. What a mess. If you do the calculation using Lowe's input, it will show that the reduction in carbon dioxide emissions is 1.4 million tonnes a year (assuming coal generation is displaced), not 5 million.

Enough! There is a lot more that could be said but that is for others. I have confined myself mainly to financial and performance aspects. I do not delude myself that my protestations will have much effect. Neither do I believe that nuclear power is likely in this country before 2030. Will Professor Lowe's recipe of renewable energies and energy efficiency with a pinch of reduced consumption give us an adequate reliable electricity supply and effective timely action on climate change? It would be a happy coincidence, but I think not. Like many things, they are essential but not sufficient.

Philip Moore

Ian Lowe

I was surprised by Philip Moore's claim that my essay *Reaction Time* was "strong on assertions but weak on factual evidence." I explicitly stated that there are different legitimate approaches to calculating the possible cost if we were to build nuclear power stations in Australia, as well as other estimates based on heroic assumptions. I used the figures in the Switkowski report because it was recent and so that I could not be accused of being biased against the nuclear industry. Moore's second paragraph underlines my case that it is possible to choose assumptions to produce a desired outcome. By using Westinghouse claims about the possible future cost and performance of a reactor that has not yet been built, he gets a capital cost of about a quarter of the historic value, a much longer lifetime and a higher capacity factor than usual, together deflating the capital cost per unit of delivered electricity by a factor of about ten or twelve. He then inflates the cost of wind by choosing a capacity factor of 20.3 per cent, whereas he accepts later in his response a more realistic figure of 37 per cent. Having fudged the comparison by about a factor of twenty, Moore concludes that the capital cost of wind is eighteen times that of nuclear. It would, as he says, take "very heroic fudging" to negate that difference if it existed, but his figures are the product of just such heroic fudging.

Building renewable-energy technologies requires energy materials and energy, but it is not true that "published estimates ... all show that [the costs] are much higher for wind and solar than for nuclear." Different assumptions lead to different conclusions. It is true that the effects of land-clearing are often ignored in estimating the costs of wind turbines or solar panels, mainly because the best sites are those already exposed to wind or sun. It would be perverse to locate a wind farm in a forest or solar panels in bushland.

It is not just my view that "nuclear power looked like a dying industry" at the turn of the century. This was a widespread feeling in the industry itself, leading to the desperate strategy of aligning itself with its traditional bitter enemies by embracing the science of climate change and attempting to re-badge nuclear power as "clean energy." It is true that nuclear power produces about 6 per cent of world energy, less than biomass (9.8 per cent) but more than hydro (2.2) and other renewables (0.7). So nuclear power is a considerable industry, but globally much more energy is provided by the mix of renewables (biomass, hydro, wind, solar etc.). The main point is that the world is going for renewables in a big way.

As far as solar hot water is concerned, I certainly wasn't "hoping nobody would bother to check" my calculations. I said households and not houses because it is not true in Queensland that every household occupies a house. Many of us live in duplexes or multi-unit constructions. The 4 million Queens-landers form about 1.6 million households, so half of these would amount to about 0.8 million hot-water systems.

A household with a solar hot-water system typically gets 90 to 95 per cent of their hot water from the sun and only 5 to 10 per cent from their back-up, usu-ally electricity, so a solar hot-water system saves 90–95 per cent of the 4 kilowatt hours or so that would otherwise be used to provide hot water. On these figures, a million hot-water systems would save about 3 million kilowatt hours per day. If a 500MW power station were built, taking distribution losses into account it would need to operate at full capacity for about eight hours every day to do the same job. It is conceivable that a first nuclear power station might do better than that, but it is also quite likely that it would not produce that much energy.

As for a construction time of "a decade or more" being "a figure that only a dedicated opponent would choose," that was the estimate in the pro-nuclear Switkowski report. Yes, it would take five to ten years to build and install a mil-lion solar hot-water systems, but that is still less time than it would take to build a nuclear power station. It would take 167 3MW wind turbines to have the same capacity as a 500MW nuclear power station and probably 400 to supply as much electricity, but hundreds of wind turbines can be built at the same time, so the construction time for equivalent capacity of wind power or other renewable supply systems would almost certainly be less than it would take to build and commission a nuclear power station. Manufacturing a million solar hot-water systems and building hundreds of wind turbines would provide meaningful work to large numbers of people – many more than would be employed if we built nuclear power stations.

Moore says that the urban myths I listed on page 27 of Reaction Time "have never been satisfactorily answered." So he apparently still thinks renewables can't be scaled up to meet our needs, even though they supply all of the electricity in Iceland and almost all in Norway, New Zealand and our state of Tasmania. He thinks they can't be deployed quickly enough, despite the clear evidence that construction times for wind turbines or solar panels are less than for nuclear power stations. And he apparently still believes that construction of wind turbines or solar panels uses more energy than they produce! That furphy was exposed fifteen years ago. This is denial on a grand scale. I did not mean electricity when I quoted the fraction of energy supplied by renewables in Sweden (one-third), Norway (half) and Iceland (three-quarters); those are the figures for total energy in those countries. They all use fossil fuels for most of their transport, so the fraction of electricity coming from renewables is much larger in every case.

I don't think I made mistakes in my explanation of the effects of discounting the future. Since this form of analysis discounts future running costs, it improves the apparent economics of a supply option with a lower capital cost and high fuel cost, such as coal, which looks better than technologies with a higher capital cost and lower running cost, such as wind or nuclear. The running cost for nuclear is much higher than wind but much less than for coal, so nuclear power and wind are disadvantaged by discounting calculations. It is often claimed that the future costs of decommissioning and waste management are included in the price of electricity from nuclear power stations and that nuclear utilities are accumulating large funds to pay these future bills. Some authorities do make allowances for these future costs, but we can't be confident that they are sufficient because nobody knows what the eventual costs will be. A documentary broadcast this year showed that decommissioning the Calder Hall reactor in the UK will take more than a hundred years, durin g all of which time the site will need to be staffed by qualified experts.

While it may be true that the imbalance in research funding between renewables and nuclear has been redressed in recent years in many overseas countries, it takes creative arithmetic to make that claim for Australia. At its height, public support of renewables research and development was only a few million dollars a year; most of those research programs are now fighting to survive. By contrast, more than $400 million was recently spent building a new reactor for the Australian Nuclear Science and Technology Organisation (ANSTO). It was commissioned last April, closed down for repairs in July and as far as I know is still out of action. We have now been funding ANSTO and its predecessor for fifty years at about $100 million a year in present terms. Apart from funding the recent supply of isotopes for high-technology medicine and measuring, that expenditure has been based on the belief that nuclear power would contribute to our future energy needs.

Moore seems to be puzzled that 426MW of gas and bio-fuels can replace a much larger amount of coal-fired generation. Combined cycle operation produces about twice as much useful energy per unit of fuel as old-fashioned steam turbines by providing process heat as well as electricity. I saw combined cycle systems in Holland thirty years ago producing 75 units of saleable energy for every 100 in the original gas, compared with about 35 for a typical power station.

In attempting to find holes in my economic analysis, I think Moore is drawing a very long bow. Nobody could accuse the Switkowski taskforce of being biased against nuclear power, but its report conceded that it is not possible to show that nuclear power is cost-effective today, even with the most charitable assumptions. But I think that argument misses the main point. I said in *Reaction Time* that the economic costs would be tolerable if that were the only way of preventing catastrophic climate change. I certainly think that it makes sense to phase out coal-fired electricity in favour of a mix of renewables, even though that will mean higher costs, for just that reason: the extra cost will be a small price to pay compared with the consequences of climate change.

I also said that the social and political costs of nuclear power did not appear to have solutions. As if to underline this point, strategic analyst Professor Paul Dibb of ANU has written about a widely circulated recent paper by former defence force chiefs in the US and Western Europe (www.csis.org/media/csis/events/080110_grand_strategy.pdf). I had recently downloaded this amazing document from the web and read it with mounting horror. The authors agree with my view that the nuclear threat today is greater than it was during the Cold War because of "rogue states" and terrorists. "They consider that nuclear war might soon become possible in an increasingly brutal world," Dibb says. So this group of ageing hawks has argued that the West should be prepared to use nuclear weapons, because that will be the only way to prevent the use of nuclear weapons! The logic is breathtaking. They think that the only way to avoid a future nuclear war is to start one now. Their paper is being considered by NATO and the Pentagon. With that sort of thinking being taken seriously, how can we possibly believe that it is worth exporting fissile material for short-term economic gains? As I argued in *Reaction Time*, there are alternatives. We can still be a role model for saner policies that slow climate change without exposing the world to needless risks.

Ian Lowe

Norman Abjorensen lectures in politics at the Australian National University. His latest book is *Leadership and the Liberal Revival: Bolte, Askin and the Post-war Ascendancy.*

Bill Bowtell was senior political adviser to the prime minister between 1994 and 1996. As senior adviser to the federal health minister, he played a significant role in the introduction of the Medicare health insurance system and was an architect of Australia's successful and well-regarded response to HIV/AIDS.

Judith Brett is the author of *Quarterly Essay 19, Relaxed and Comfortable: The Liberal Party's Australia, Robert Menzies' Forgotten People* and *Australian Liberals and the Moral Middle Class: From Alfred Deakin to John Howard.* A regular commentator for *The Monthly,* she is professor of politics at La Trobe University.

Rebecca Huntley has worked as an academic and political staffer and is now a social researcher with Ipsos Mackay. She is the author of *The World According to Y: Inside the New Adult Generation.* Her next book, about the food cultures of Australia, will be published in September 2008.

Tony Kevin, a former Australian diplomat (1968–98), is the author of *A Certain Maritime Incident: the Sinking of SIEV X* and *Walking the Camino.*

Ian Lowe is emeritus professor of science, technology and society at Griffith University and president of the Australian Conservation Foundation. He studied engineering and science at the University of New South Wales and earned his doctorate in physics from the University of York. He is the author of many books, including *A Big Fix* and *Living in the Hothouse.*

Anne Manne is a regular contributor to *The Age* and *The Monthly.* Her book *Motherhood: How Should We Care for Our Children?* was shortlisted for the 2006 Walkley non-fiction prize. She has written widely on feminism, motherhood, childcare, family policy, fertility and related issues.

Philip Moore worked for thirty years in nuclear research at the Australian Atomic Energy Commission and the Australian Nuclear Science and Technology Organisation. For some years he represented Australia and reported on nuclear matters in Asia, the UK and Western Europe, and for the OECD Nuclear Energy Agency.

Subscribe to Quarterly Essay

POST OR FAX THIS FORM TO: Quarterly Essay, Reply Paid 79448, Melbourne VIC 3000
Freecall: 1800 077 514 **Fax:** 61 3 9654 2290 **Email:** subscribe@blackincbooks.com

....

SUBSCRIPTIONS Receive a discount and never miss an issue. Mailed direct to your door.

1 year subscription (4 issues): $49 a year within Australia incl. GST. Outside Australia $79.

2 year subscription (8 issues): $95 a year within Australia incl. GST. Outside Australia $155.

* All prices include postage and handling.

....

BACK ISSUES Please add $2.50 postage and handling to your order (or $8.00 for overseas orders).

☐ **QE 1** ($9.95) Robert Manne *In Denial*
☐ **QE 2** ($9.95) John Birmingham *Appeasing Jakarta*
☐ **QE 4** ($9.95) Don Watson *Rabbit Syndrome*
☐ **QE 5** ($11.95) Mungo MacCallum *Girt by Sea*
☐ **QE 6** ($11.95) John Button *Beyond Belief*
☐ **QE 7** ($11.95) John Martinkus *Paradise Betrayed*
☐ **QE 8** ($11.95) Amanda Lohrey *Groundswell*
☐ **QE 10** ($12.95) Gideon Haigh *Bad Company*
☐ **QE 11** ($12.95) Germaine Greer *Whitefella Jump Up*
☐ **QE 12** ($12.95) David Malouf *Made in England*
☐ **QE 13** ($12.95) Robert Manne with David Corlett *Sending Them Home*
☐ **QE 14** ($13.95) Paul McGeough *Mission Impossible*
☐ **QE 15** ($13.95) Margaret Simons *Latham's World*
☐ **QE 16** ($13.95) Raimond Gaita *Breach of Trust*
☐ **QE 17** ($13.95) John Hirst *'Kangaroo Court'*
☐ **QE 18** ($13.95) Gail Bell *The Worried Well*
☐ **QE 19** ($14.95) Judith Brett *Relaxed and Comfortable*
☐ **QE 20** ($14.95) John Birmingham *A Time for War*
☐ **QE 21** ($14.95) Clive Hamilton *What's Left?*
☐ **QE 22** ($14.95) Amanda Lohrey *Voting for Jesus*
☐ **QE 23** ($14.95) Inga Clendinnen *The History Question*
☐ **QE 24** ($14.95) Robyn Davidson *No Fixed Address*
☐ **QE 25** ($14.95) Peter Hartcher *Bipolar Nation*
☐ **QE 26** ($14.95) David Marr *His Master's Voice*
☐ **QE 27** ($14.95) Ian Lowe *Reaction Time*
☐ **QE 28** ($14.95) Judith Brett *Exit Right*

....

PAYMENT DETAILS I enclose a cheque/money order made out to Schwartz Publishing Pty Ltd.
Please debit my credit card (Mastercard, Visa or Bankcard accepted).

Card No. ☐☐☐☐ ☐☐☐☐ ☐☐☐☐ ☐☐☐☐ ☐☐☐☐

Expiry date   /   Amount $

Cardholder's name   Signature

Name

Address

Email

Subscribe online at **www.quarterlyessay.com**

www.ingramcontent.com/pod-product-compliance
Lightning Source LLC
Chambersburg PA
CBHW081401270326
41930CB00015B/3379